HEY!
DO I NEED
A VA?

A How-to Guide to Find,
Hire and Work With a Virtual Assistant

Rachael Davila

HEY!
DO I NEED A VA?

A How-to Guide to Find,
Hire and Work With a Virtual Assistant

To request permissions, contact the author at:
hello@extrahandsva.com

Published by Pomegraf Editing & Book Development
Lakeside, California

Cover Design by Above Talent Creation
Editing by Elizabeth Bercovici, Magical Storytelling
Interior & Type Layout by Jessica Brodkin Webb

The information in this book is based on the author's knowledge, experience and opinions. The methods described in this book are not intended to be a definitive set of instructions. You may discover other methods and materials to accomplish the same end result. Your results my differ.

ISBN 979-8-9990735-1-8

Early Praise For

HEY!
DO I NEED
A VA?

A How-to Guide to Find,
Hire and Work With a Virtual Assistant

♥

"Rachael Davila builds on her years of experience as a business owner supporting other business owners to offer tangible, practical advice on hiring a virtual assistant. Think of this as a user guide to the before, during and after of the VA relationship. You'll learn how VAs can help you do your best work, and how to make the best use of their skills as well. As a longtime client of Rachael's, it's a treat to see her sharing her thoughtfulness with a broader audience in book form!"

— Alan Heymann, Peaceful Direction

"This book is a must-have for any entrepreneur who's ready to stop spinning their wheels and start building a business with support. Rachael has created a thoughtful, actionable guide that walks you step-by-step through the process of finding and working with the right virtual assistant or remote support. Her years of experience working with clients and mentoring others in the industry, has given her such a wealth of information that she shares so openly.

What makes this book truly transformational are the practical, actionable tools— insightful exercises, reflection prompts, and smart interview questions— that help you make confident, aligned decisions. If you're ready to grow your business with the right help by your side— start here."

— Bree BV, BeeVee Pro

To My Dad, Nowell Wisch—

My first client;

My greatest support;

My loudest cheerleader.

– Contents –

– Introduction –

"Hire a Virtual Assistant." ... "Just outsource it!"

You've likely heard a version of these suggestions but don't actually know what to do with them. Where do you start? Who do you call? Do you take out an ad on Google or hire a skywriter to plaster your need for a Virtual Assistant (VA) across the clouds with the hope that the right someone is looking up?

Or you found someone who says they are a virtual assistant but you're stuck in indecision limbo and afraid to take the leap and trust your business to anyone (let alone the wrong support person).

I know how you feel because I've been there.

Let me just say that even though I've been a virtual assistant since 2005, when the moment came for me to hire my own support person, my years of experience did not make things any easier. In fact, I think it made it harder.

I had expectations of what I hoped to find in a VA that didn't come true. I had to release control that I'd spent years holding onto with a tight grip. I had to shift my mindset from "but I can do this myself" to "it's better for everyone if I let my assistant do it".

Going through this journey is why I shifted my business from being a VA who solely does the work to helping business owners learn what they need to know when they start asking themselves, "Hey! Do I Need a VA?".

Preparing to bring on a team member (especially a virtual one) takes time and effort. This book is all about taking the knowledge I've acquired from helping hundreds of clients as a VA and my own experience of shifting from doer to client to guide you through the process of confidently finding, hiring and working with a VA.

Before we begin, let me tell you who I am and a little about my journey...

My Story

I am Rachael Davila. I am the proud owner of *Extra Hands! Virtual Assistance*, a wife, a mother of two, a daughter, a sister and a friend. I've always loved helping people. My mom was a teacher and I would help her grade papers and organize her classroom at the beginning of every school year. I always thought I would become a teacher. However, in college I discovered my talents lay, not in front of a classroom, but behind the scenes. I tried many different departments until I found Stage Management. A stage manager is the administrative assistant for a theater production. I loved being the hub of the wheel, assisting the director and making sure their vision stayed the course over a multi-week run.

Those skills transferred nicely to the role of administrative assistant. I worked for my dad, a traveling salesman, a non-profit and a corporation before finding my true career in virtual assistance.

At the end of 2004, my corporate job announced it was downsizing all the administrative staff. My kids were young and I wanted more flexibility than a 7-4 job. I explored options like event planner and professional organizer. Neither were perfect. There were elements of both that I was iffy on. With a young family and an early bedtime, organizing worked better for my family with no late nights due to events.

One day, while helping a friend organize her office, she suggested I create a business name. An internet search for the name I liked yielded a website for a Virtual Assistant. After reading through the entire site, I was enchanted. Two decades later I don't remember what exactly was written on the webpage but it made me reach out to learn more. She lived near me in San Diego and not only agreed to talk with me but spent over an hour sharing what she did, how she started and how I could do it too. It was magical. Everything she shared with me felt exactly like what I wanted to do.

I asked if she was worried about me starting my own VA business and she just laughed. She told me she didn't see us as competition because we each had our own skills and voices and therefore wouldn't be competing for the same clients.

During that conversation, I learned that being a virtual assistant wasn't just about doing the admin work. It was a business and needed to be treated as one. I signed up for the Virtual Training Program at AssistU to learn how to establish myself as a business owner. After 20 weeks and a 3 day exam I opened my virtual doors officially in June 2005.

Over the last two decades, I've seen that everything that VA said to me is true. VAs are not in competition with each other. I interact with VAs all the time and it's amazing to see that we may work in the same programs but none of us do it the exact same way nor do we run our businesses the same.

There are enough clients to go around and if I'm not the right fit, I can offer connections to someone who might be. It's my belief that creating long-lasting VA/Client relationships is all about finding the right fit and the right partner for your business instead of just someone to do the work.

When the fit is right, magic happens. It ripples outward. This allows my clients to show up as the star of their production and shine for their audience. I become the stage manager and take over the tasks that stop them from working in their Zone of Genius[1] so they can show up as their best selves. To see my clients shine fills my heart with joy. When my clients succeed, I succeed. I love that kind of ripple effect.

1- "The Big Leap" by Çay Hendricks explains these zones.

From Doer to Client

By all accounts, I am successful. I have made it long past the 5-year threshold in which most businesses fail. I've worked with ideal clients, weathered the ups and downs of industry shifts, worked through my issues of imposter syndrome and questioned whether I am worth what I charge. My chest swells with pride sometimes knowing I have beaten the odds.

Until 2021, I helped my clients focus on growing their businesses but played small when it came to my own. For most of my career, whenever I thought of a successful full-time practice, I envisioned myself as a solo player billing 60-80 hours a month. In the fall of 2021, I hit that hourly goal and it nearly killed me. My health was affected because I wasn't taking care of myself and had no work-life balance.

That was the moment I realized I couldn't keep going the way I had been and the vision for my business fundamentally shifted. I was not prepared for the level of success I had achieved and it scared me. I didn't want to do everything for my clients with no time left over for me. I loved working with my clients. I loved brainstorming, collaborating and coaching them from their vision to reality. I was just overwhelmed with doing all the little tasks that came with it.

Sound familiar? I know! In my head, I was starting to sound like one of my clients.

I wasn't sure I could ask for help let alone release enough

control or let go of my perfectionism to allow someone to help me. The tasks were mine to do and I could do them.

Succeeding in my goal of a full time practice had not been the blissful experience I had imagined. The experience taught me a very valuable lesson that just because I can do it doesn't mean I should. If I was going to be successful, it wasn't going to look like I had once imagined. The type of business I envisioned was possible but not on my own.

It took an outside perspective to offer a solution. A coach friend suggested I hire my own VA to help me build a foundation so I could scale my business in a healthier way.

A VA with a VA? It seemed funny at first. Rather than dismiss it out of hand, I let the idea marinate. Three months later, hiring a VA didn't feel so scary.

I decided I was ready to walk my talk and jump into the experience. Like many clients, I didn't know what I didn't know. I figured my VA would guide me the way I always guided my clients. I didn't do any of the pre-work I'm going to encourage you to do. Instead, I casually mentioned I was looking for a VA in one of my accountability groups.

That same afternoon I got an email from a friend asking if I would consider working with her high school senior who was looking for a part-time job. I said yes on the spot. I didn't even do an interview. I hired a 17 year old with great artistic and graphic design skills who wanted to be a VA.

That meant they had zero VA experience and no knowledge on how to guide the relationship. I found myself as a mentor, guide and client which was all new territory for me. However, I was sure we could figure it out together.

Right away I started to hand off small but important things to my VA. They were things I didn't want to do. There was ease in giving them to my VA and relief when they were completed with only minor adjustments needed. It felt like we were building trust right off the bat. Then the momentum stalled because of me.

I found myself giving into my perfectionism. I was tweaking tiny things, hoarding tasks and generally not utilizing my VA. Instead of asking for work, they were content to wait until I gave them something to do.

I had some learning to do about myself and how I was showing up as a leader. Once I could finally verbalize my needs, my VA was happy to step up and pull tasks out of my clutches.

The Universe likes to fill a void and handing things off to my VA created a big one for me. The creative gates opened and ideas for a whole new direction poured out of me. It was overwhelming but in a good way. With my newly cleared time, I was able to redo my website, start a podcast, expand my social media messaging with videos and eventually write this book.

For the first time, I understood what it felt like to be a client. I felt the fear, stepped into courage and enjoyed the freedom of handing things off. I felt the feelings of anxiety and safety and excitement to try new things. I took a risk and built something big because I had a team to support me and hold me accountable.

It is my hope that through the chapters in this book, you will peel back the layers of any fear and worry you have to lay down the foundation needed to find the right fit for you and your business.

This is not a one-size-fits-all journey but if you go on it with me, I know you will walk away with the answers you need to find the support that will help you grow bigger than you could ever imagine.

With a bit of work on your part, we can make magic happen and when you ask yourself, "Hey! Do I Need a VA?" you will know with certainty.

– Warmly, Rachael

– How To Use This Book –

Just like no two VAs are alike, no two readers are alike. This book is not designed with a one-size-fits-all mentality. This book is intended to be informational to an audience who is looking to create long-term relationships with virtual support.

There is no right or wrong way to use this book. You get to decide if you want to use it as a workbook, a guide or keep it only for reference.

Inside you will find a lot of useful information on how to find, hire and work with a virtual assistant. It's not in my nature to talk theory. I talk action. I learn better if I do the steps as I go but not everyone is like me... and that's okay.

Some chapters are reading chapters with information to make you think. Others are action chapters with Take Action exercises to complete. At the end of each chapter are Recap: Key Points summaries and Journal Prompts to ponder. Look for these images to guide you:

Take Action: Action Steps

Recap: Key Points: Chapter Summaries

Journal Prompts: Questions to Ponder

My recommendation is if you are actively considering working with a virtual assistant or believe you will be looking in the next couple of months, take the time to do the exercises found in the chapters.

Even if you read the whole book *without* doing the exercises, you will still gain a lot and then you can come back when you're ready. It may feel like a lot of work. It is and so is the journey to find the right VA. Believe me when I say that it's well worth your time and effort.

Along the way, I reference books and authors who helped me on my journey. As of this printing, they can all be found on Amazon but you can also check your local library or purchase them through your retailer of choice.

The full bibliography and footnote information can be found on my website where I set up a page with all of the resources, along with current links as of this printing. You can find that Resources webpage at **https:// extrahandsva.com/resources/**

Also found on the Resources page are the worksheets and handouts described in the exercises. You can download individual pages or grab the full workbook. Please note that downloading the documents is optional. You can always use a blank sheet of paper, notebook or journal. All the PDFs are fillable so you can type your responses if that is how you work best.

If you get to the end of the book and decide it's all too much to do alone, I can help! Whether you're looking for referrals, want more guidance or prefer a customized experience, I offer options for everyone and you can learn more about working together at www.ExtraHandsVA.com.

Let's get started!

Chapter One

How Do I Know If I'm Ready?

"The journey of a thousand miles begins with a single step." — Chinese proverb

If you're asking "How do I know if I'm ready?" then I would say you're already on the journey. Every goal we set out to accomplish becomes a parallel journey.

There is the outer journey which is the visible goal we tell others about like hiring a VA, writing a book or hosting a workshop.

Then there is the inner journey. This isn't a visible, tangible change. It is an opportunity to grow, stretch and adjust our mindset to become the person who can reach our goals. The inner journey often requires us to release old beliefs, form new habits, and change how we look at our lives and businesses.

This chapter is about asking the tough questions before you ever set foot on the path.

Have you hit your "Not This" moment?

At some point in time, we all hit a moment when we're done. We can no longer live life the way we're currently living. We face a crossroads where we need to choose to make a change or wilt away.

That is a "Not This" moment.

I got that term from a Facebook post entitled "Not This" by Elizabeth Gilbert.[1] She wrote, "Most of us, at some point in our lives... will have to face a terrible moment in which we realize that we have somehow ended up in the wrong place... I call this moment of realization: NOT THIS."

"Not This" moments are the starting point. It's when the decision is made for something better. It's the trigger and the prompt that something is wrong and we need to do something different.

For some people, their "Not This" moment is the impetus they need to create better habits or recognize they can't say yes to every social event that comes their way or that it is finally time to hire help. They use their "Not This" moments to start clearing their pebbles and make real lasting change.

Looking back, I recognize many "Not This" moments in my life. Each one was pivotal to me becoming the person I am today and each one scared me enough to know there was no going back.

1- *"Not This"* by Elizabeth Gilbert.

Here is how these moments showed up for me:

- As a stress-filled decision to stay or go during a corporate downsizing.
- Having a "do we get a divorce" conversation with my husband.
- Feeling alone in a crowd of people having the same shallow conversations.
- Getting diagnosed with Diabetes.
- Realizing that the changes I needed to make start with me and I can't change anyone but myself.

After each "Not This" moment, I learned to:

- Prioritize events and engagements with people that feel right for me.
- Do the hard soul searching work to uncover the hidden barriers I'd placed between me and success.
- Release years of negative thoughts about what I deserved or what I was capable of achieving in order to make real progress on my goals.
- Focus on my own actions and habits to build a business I'm proud of.
- Shift away from who I used to be and honor the person I am becoming. I am more than a mother, a wife, and a sister. I am someone with my own dreams and desires!

If you're standing at a crossroads and "Not This" is filling you up, that's a good thing in my opinion because it means you're ready to make a change.

Use your "Not This" moment to:

- Gain clarity on what you don't want so you can get clear on what you do.

- Prioritize the changes you want to make in your life.

- Make a plan to create small changes in your daily life to reach those priority goals.

- Get clear on WHY you're making the changes in your life and what you envision for the outcome.

Not all "Not This" moments are breaking points. What if it's a dreaming point? Maybe it's finally time to dust off the goals and projects you've been hiding away in your soul. Those things that only you can do for the world. Maybe you have a knowing that with the right partner on your side you can do bigger and better things or maybe it's the difference between a "Not This" voice that's a shout vs a whisper.

You DESERVE to have what is on the other side of "Not This."

Working through my "Not This" moments, I realized I deserved to love all the events on my calendar. I deserved to work in my Zone of Genius. I deserved my success and a life of ease.

YOU deserve all that too and you don't need to do it alone.

Before we get started on how to find a VA, let's first discuss signs that you may not be ready to start the journey at this time—

You don't have a steady income or money saved to pay for help.

A common dilemma clients face is needing VA services to help grow their businesses but not earning a sufficient income or having money saved to pay for those services. Budgeting and prioritizing tasks can help bridge this gap but if funds aren't available, it's a sign you may need to wait and save.

You don't have clear business goals or know what help you need.

A VA can help with nearly anything but we're not mind readers. VA/client partnerships require guidance and leadership. Without clear directions from you, a VA can only do so much to support your vision. VAs look to their clients to lead the way on their business goals and objectives for working together. If you're unclear about where you want your business to go and how a VA can contribute to your goals, that's another sign that you might not be ready.

If getting clear on your goals and charting out a direction to go is the support you need, there are collaborative VAs who specialize in strategy and planning. It's perfectly fine to start working with this type of VA to create the foundational support and goal setting before hiring a doer VA to help you implement your vision.

You might need someone other than a VA.

Although the term virtual assistant has been thrown around as the catch-all for virtual business support, a VA may not be the right fit for you. Depending on your needs, you may want to look for a specialist, personal assistant or employee.

Depending on your task list and managing style, you may want someone in person or need more time than most VAs can offer. In terms of billable hours, VAs typically don't work more than 40 hours per month for a single client especially for compliance reasons in American states like California because exceeding 40 hours would categorize the VA as an employee.

If you need someone full-time, on-site and available for immediate assistance or if you're someone who prefers face-to-face interactions with your support staff, an in-office assistant, employee or temporary staff member might be a better fit.

You don't have time to invest in the relationship.

The first few months of working together builds the foundation of the VA/Client relationship. It takes an investment of time and communication to get to a place of trust. If you can't or won't dedicate time to checking in, answering questions, and guiding your VA, you may want to reconsider.

You work to emergencies and need someone at your beck-and-call.

Emergencies and last minute projects are a reality in any business but if you're the type who is always waiting until the last minute or you expect fast results, a VA may not be the right fit for you. These types of situations are "working to emergencies."

Because VAs work with multiple clients, it's not realistic to expect them to be readily available whenever a client needs them. Most will communicate their work schedules and the best way for clients to reach them but they often try to pad deliverables to fit into their workload and plan accordingly.

If you've looked at these and feel like they don't apply to you, maybe you're more ready than you thought. Still, is the risk worth taking?

Business owners make difficult choices every day. It comes with the territory of creating something all our own. One of the biggest risks we take when our load becomes too big is to hire help.

The risk I see most potential clients take isn't hiring a VA but going into the process blind on how to find the right fit.

It doesn't matter how awesome a particular VA is. Working with another person who is most likely someone you don't know can be scary. There is no way to know if anything they say is true until you're in the middle of a project. *Risky.*

No matter how detailed the interview process, you're handing over sensitive information like passwords and credit card numbers. *Risky.*

You're entrusting your brand and reputation to the finished product of any task you hand off. *Risky.*

There is always the chance that you'll end up spending more time training or fixing mistakes than freeing up your time. *Risky.*

Trust is always risky.

There are some ways to mitigate your risk and we will go through them in more detail throughout the book but here are a few tips to get you started.

- **Get clear on what qualities you are looking for in a support person:** Many times potential clients focus so much on their task list that they don't consider more important aspects of what they really need. Finding someone to do a task isn't the risky part. It's more risky to believe you are hiring a competent VA who can do everything you asked only to discover they need more hand holding than you expected.

- **Work with someone you know or who comes as a referral:** Most potential clients who come to me are usually referrals. We've engaged in some way through networking events or social media. There is a level of established connection that gives a feeling of comfort for them to reach out and ask questions. When looking for a virtual assistant, reach out to your community and get referrals. It's okay to ask the person giving the referral why they feel it's a good fit.

- **Start slow and build trust:** It's okay to start with a trial period to feel each other out. Start with easy and non-critical projects to see how those get handled. Build from there or gracefully end the relationship. Taking a risk on someone doesn't mean the relationship is set in stone. You both have the right to walk away if the return isn't what you expected.

If you're going to take the risk of letting somebody into your business, you should do the hard work to discover what it is you actually need and then find the person who can do it. This book is all about setting you up for success.

In business there are risks worth taking. Are you ready to take the risk?

When I first considered hiring my own VA, I didn't know what I didn't know. It took me three months to take the leap. When I made the decision to go for it, I jumped in without looking.

My experience in asking for help wasn't great. I was often the kid in group projects who took on more work rather than asking for help. Whenever I did ask for help, I felt like my requests were a burden or else I had to micromanage to get things done. I still haven't figured out how to ask my kids to help and not feel like a nag.

I definitely didn't want to feel that way with someone I was paying to help me.

Then the other thoughts rolled in.

Who would I find to do the work as good as I did?

Who would take care of my clients to the quality I demanded of myself?

How would I pay for someone else's time and still meet my own expenses?

The list went on and on.

Can you relate?

Going through the process, I can tell you it is scary. That is probably why many clients give up working with a VA. Fear of the unknown can make any situation feel bigger and more overwhelming.

"Can you keep going the way you are?"

— LeAnn Erimli, Handling Business

Hiring a VA isn't just about offloading tasks. It's about creating space for growth and creativity. A good VA becomes a partner who supports your vision and helps you focus on what truly matters. If you're burned out doing things that drain you, when do you have time to do the tasks you're passionate about? What about the ones that grow your business?

Virtual assistants are business partners. They're not formally part of your business but they have a vested interest in helping you grow. When you're successful, they're successful!

Shifting your mindset from solopreneur to teampreneur takes some work. It doesn't happen overnight and it may not happen until you start working with someone. Learning as you go may be the only way to get started.

Before you start the search, ask yourself some deep questions. Be honest with yourself.

- **What gaps do you have in your business?** In all good relationships, opposites attract. A VA is supposed to complement you. They are not going to step in to do the parts of your business that you are passionate about. They are going to take over those tasks that you dread but are vital to driving your business forward. These are your gaps.

  It's not just the task gap either. Are you a visionary who needs accountability to execute your vision or do you easily get distracted and need someone to keep you focused? Are you exhausted from always working to the point that a task becomes an emergency? Do you need someone to create realistic timelines for you to get things done or someone to talk you down from the ledge when you start spiraling with overthinking? Do you need a calming presence to counteract your anxiety? Do you need support with your business to allow more time for life?

  What gaps have you tolerated in yourself and your business that no longer serve you and what are you ready to change?

- **Have you ever managed people or worked with an assistant before? What worked and what didn't?** I believe running a family counts as managing people although managing my VA is way easier than getting my kids to do anything. I've been a teacher, committee member, and on the board of a couple of organizations. None of these management roles actually prepared me to lead a co-worker.

- **Why is now the right time for you to work with a virtual assistant?** Look at the reasons you are thinking about it now. Write them down. What is going on in your life or business that is driving your interest to get help? Have you hit your breaking point? Are you ready to dream bigger with the right helper?

  It's okay to start where you are and grow as you gain comfort in the process.

- **Get Clear on Your *WHY*—** Determining why you are looking for help in the first place sets the course for everything. These reasons will keep you on track when things get rough. You need to have an idea and a direction for your business or working with a VA will only be busy work. Taking the time to clarify your why takes work and practice. I can say from experience and client testimonials that the process is worth it.

  I introduced a client to a VA to help him with increasing a social media presence. In our follow up call, the client realized that he wasn't ready to work with a VA on social media because he wasn't sure what parts of his business he wanted to focus on. He had no clarity on his content and therefore couldn't direct the VA on what to create. Before he could start with a VA, the client needed to get clear on why he was posting to social media in the first place.

While most of the topics we'll discuss in the book are logical and focused on implementation, this mindset piece is emotional and only something you can work on.

Talking it through with a trusted friend or colleague may help you discover what your hidden blocks are or highlight any limiting beliefs you may carry about you deserving to get the help and support you need to grow your business. It may help to go through the rest of the book and come back to this point or feel free to reach out to me for coaching.

Lots of people have gone through the process and though it may feel a little painful or overwhelming, just know you are not alone.

You got this!

You can do hard things!

You can find the right support for you and your needs.

Let's start figuring out what those are.

Recap: Key Points

If you're asking whether you're ready to hire a VA, you're likely already on the journey.

- However, you may not be ready if you don't have steady income, clear business goals, or a defined need for VA support.

- Ensure you have the financial resources to pay for VA services and a clear understanding of your business goals. Without clarity, it's difficult to direct a VA effectively.

- A VA may not always be the right solution. If you need full-time, in-person, or specialized support, consider other options like hiring employees or specialists.

- Building a strong VA-client relationship requires time and communication especially in the beginning. Without this investment, the partnership may not thrive.

- Shifting from a solopreneur to a teampreneur mindset can be challenging. Trusting a VA to take over tasks and letting go of perfectionism is key to growth both personally and in your business.

- To determine if now is the right time to hire a VA, reflect on the gaps in your business and what you're tolerating. If your "why" is clear and strong, the process can lead to significant growth.

Journal Prompts

☺ What are my gaps?

☺ What are my blocks and who do I need to become to overcome them?

☺ Am I actually ready to hire someone?

Chapter Two

Your Hand-Off List

Like I said in the "How to use this book" section, some chapters are for reading and others are for doing. This is a doing chapter and it is a long one with multiple exercises that may feel overwhelming.

You can read through the whole chapter and then come back to do the exercises or you can do them along the way. If necessary, give yourself some grace and take a break. I promise I'll still be here when you're ready to come back!

Creating Your Hand-off List

Most potential clients' main focus when looking to work with a virtual assistant is to hand off tasks they don't want to do. Figuring out this hand-off list is important but only the first step.

If you're thinking, "I know I need help but I don't know what help I need," let me put your mind at ease. You don't need to have all the answers.

During those initial conversations with your VA, you will work together to create a plan to work through the tasks most important to you and your business goals. As you get to know each other, additional answers will start to emerge.

Lots of clients go into the process thinking that they have to hand off everything to a VA which is not true. Within the flow of any task, project, or process, there are things that you like doing and those that you don't.

For example, my colleague LeAnn and I are the perfect yin and yang to each other's businesses. She is the techie VA while I'm more creative. She is always telling me that I can't break the internet because she loves all things technical. I, on the other hand, have a healthy (or not so healthy) fear of technology that I don't understand. I turn to LeAnn whenever I come across a task that isn't in my Zone of Genius. In the same way, LeAnn doesn't feel she is as creative as me so she hands off tasks that fall into that category in her mind. We fill in each other's gaps.

In order to find the right fit for your business, you need to have an initial idea of what you're looking for. Let me ask you:

- Why did you start your business in the first place?
- What do you enjoy most about what you're doing?
- What is getting in your way of doing that?
- What do you wish somebody would take off your plate?
- What is your biggest pain point?
- What is going on in your business that led you to consider working with a VA in the first place?

Wherever possible, those tasks you don't love doing become your hand-off list.

Take Action

Let's Create Your Hand-Off List

Instead of just talking about a hand-off list, let's create yours. There are lots of ways you could tackle this, but here is the process I take my clients through.

Step One: Collect Your Thoughts

If you're anything like me, your brain is full of ideas, plans, and dreams. Sometimes those ideas get jotted down on Post-it notes, random scraps of paper, digital files, or in various notebooks. Mostly, they're just swirling around your head making it hard to think straight let alone focus on your goals.

In her book, The Life Changing Magic of Not Giving a F*@k, Sarah Knight uses the term Brain Dump to describe the process of emptying your brain onto paper.

Imagine your head is an office with overflowing papers piled high on a desk and spilling out of filing cabinets. A Brain Dump entails collecting all those imaginary notes and clearing out your mental office by collecting your thoughts on paper.

Download the **Brain Dump** worksheet from the Resources webpage or grab paper and a pen, get comfortable and take a deep breath. Put pen to paper and start unloading everything that comes to mind.

Don't edit yourself.

Don't worry if you repeat the same items.

Don't worry if it's personal or business ideas, projects or to-do tasks.

Just write down everything that comes to mind.

The first time I did this, it took me almost 30 minutes to empty my head. I had goals, to-dos, wishes and fears. I had my kids' doctor appointments and plans for my daughter's Bat Mitzvah (a year away) and all things in between. With practice, I can now clear my head in less than 10 minutes.

When you start, I recommend setting a 20 minute timer to give yourself a time limit. You want to fully empty your head but don't want to overthink it. There is no right or wrong way to do this! It takes as long as it takes.

In all fairness, I will warn you that it can feel like a door that has been locked is now open and you can't close it again. Keep the list handy because once you start this process, the clearing can become an avalanche of stray thoughts that continue to show up for days or weeks. You might be surprised by what comes up. It's like finding lost treasure or little items that fall behind the filing cabinet or get pushed to the back of the desk drawer.

The important thing is to get the bulk of what is in your head out and onto paper so you can see your thoughts in black and white. Additionally, your head is not the only place you store ideas. Remember those Post-its, slips of paper and notebooks scattered around? Grab everything you can find and consolidate those thoughts and ideas onto your list. Most likely those items are already listed.

Goals

Everyone has goals. Some are big and some are small. Some they are already working on and others are so overwhelming that they are spoken as a wistful, "someday".

Setting a goal is easy but implementing a goal often feels

impossible. Why? Because we can't "poof" a goal into being. A goal is an outcome, an aspiration, or a dream that takes a series of actions, tasks, and behavior changes to make happen.

To reach a goal, we need to break it down into milestones, projects, single-action steps and tiny habits.

Taking the time to work through your goals to get down to those single-action steps can be helpful in determining what items make it to your to-do list and what can be handed off. We will tackle that second step in a bit but for now, all you need to do is write down your goals. Use the **Goals List** worksheet on the Resources webpage or add to your brain dump list. These can be personal or professional.

Even if you don't do all the exercises the first time you go through this book, pause and write down what came to mind as you were reading this section about goals. Don't procrastinate because your goals are important! More than likely they are the reasons you got into business in the first place and are usually the tasks that get shunted aside. They deserve your attention and you deserve to give time and energy to your passions.

If you still feel like you're missing something and need help figuring out what additional tasks you might want to hand off, download **200+ Services A Virtual Assistant Offers** from the Resources webpage. You can look through the PDF and jot down any additional ideas that maybe you didn't think about. Most likely these items are the "one day" tasks you would love help with but never thought you could get help with.

Procrastinations and Tolerations

It's easy to get caught up in the day-to-day tasks required to run a business and by doing so, make little progress on our overall goals. Overwhelm often shows up as **procrastinations** and **tolerations**.

Procrastinations are things that we really want to get done but something is blocking our way. These tend to be projects or tasks we keep pushing off until we start to feel bad about not completing them like that line item on your to-do list that always gets pushed to the next day, week, or month.

Tolerations are items, situations, or to-do tasks that bug us but not enough for us to do anything about them. We put up with them because they don't have a direct negative impact on us like walking past a sock on the floor but not picking it up or grabbing a dead pen and throwing it back in the drawer rather than throwing it out.

Ignoring procrastinations and tolerations eventually takes up time, energy, and resources. Lack of energy, motivation and time often contributes to small tolerations turning into big procrastinations. Identifying these in your life and working to eliminate them can reduce overwhelm and anxiety, give you more energy, create a sense of calm, and unclutter your mental space.

Are any tasks on your brain dump procrastinations or tolerations? If yes, don't beat yourself up. Sometimes it's hard to separate the guilt or shame of not getting something done quickly but there is always a reason for it. This reason most likely has nothing to do with your ability to accomplish it. Instead it is something that you may or may not have control over. Look at those items with curiosity rather than judgment.

Maybe you're suffering from perfectionism or the task is overwhelming. Perhaps you need to learn something first (or think you do) or have time blindness and incorrectly estimate how long the task will take or forget other tasks that need completion first. Is it just not the right time? Are you not the right person to do it?

If you have any thoughts in your mental office that you feel are procrastinations or tolerations, write them on your brain dump or use the **Procrastinations and Tolerations** handout on the Resources webpage. It's okay if they are personal or business. If you can identify the reason(s), jot that down too.

My goal to create a podcast was a procrastination item on my to-do list for 2 years. Sharing my office space with my daughter meant that I had no privacy or uninterrupted quiet time. I would not have been able to record an episode with ease. When my shoffice (shed-office) was built and I finally had my own space, it was time to bring that dream to life.

The Silent To-Do List

Also, consider the hidden expenditures not usually associated with our tasks: the Silent To-Dos.

In his book Goodbye, Things, Fumio Sasaki says *"every single material item in your house is sending out a message."* I would argue that the same is true for your to-do list.

Just as dishes piled in the sink say "wash me, dry me," newsletters say "research me, find time to write creatively" and events say "prepare for me, participate in me, and don't forget to follow up with those people you met at the event".

Everything on your to-do list or calendar (whether personal or business) is sending these silent and subconscious messages. It's why going on vacation is so relaxing. We often leave our computer or work at home and we can't hear any of our stuff crying out to be managed!

Everything you want to do has a silent to-do list attached.

A program you want to create doesn't just require a 90-minute presentation. It is time to create the content and design slides, send out promotional emails and develop social media posts. It is time to practice and don't forget the energy expended to show up as well as the energy to refill reserves afterward.

Another example is back to back client calls that require time to schedule, prepare and follow up afterward and the mental shift to transition from one call to another. A 15-minute call requires far more than 15 minutes of your time.

When it comes to your task list, project or goal, it's important to consider these hidden expenditures and silent to-dos. Look at your brain dump list and write down any realistic additions for each of these tasks.

If you're looking at your brain dump list and getting anxious about all the things you see listed, don't worry! This list is not your to-do list. You do not need to take any action on these tasks at this moment. This is simply a list of all the things that have been inside you (possibly for years). If it's long, it is no wonder you're exhausted and looking for help.

If this all seems like a lot to handle, this is a good point to pause and take a break. When you come back, I'll show you one way to organize your thoughts into a prioritized hand-off list.

Step Two: Organize Your Thoughts

Now it's time to take your brain dump list and organize it. This step aims to create a detailed list of the priorities that are top of mind.

One reason for procrastination is that the task is too big and overwhelming. Too often we put a task on our to-do list that seems like it's a single-action task but really it's multiple steps. For instance, let's look at "Start a newsletter".

Sounds simple right?

When you start breaking it down to its individual tasks, there are at least 19 steps. I know because I counted. If you're interested here are some of those subtasks:

1. *Figure out the email platform.*
2. *Set up sign up format (website, blog, social media link).*
3. *Set up an account.*
4. *Design template.*
5. *Design email header.*
6. *Create your free gift.*
7. *Set up email automation for free gift.*
8. *Spread the word about the newsletter.*
9. *Plan content.*
10. *Write content.*
11. *Edit content.*
12. *Collect/design graphics.*
13. *Format content.*
14. *Preview email.*
15. *Test email links.*
16. *Schedule email.*
17. *Check analytics.*
18. *Post notifications to social media.*
19. *Repeat.*

Or, using this example, what if adding a newsletter is a new idea for your marketing plan and not in your wheelhouse at all? As you're thinking of your hand-off list, if the whole idea is too scary, write down "start a newsletter" on your list. If you'd like to be more involved in the process, the right VA can help you break down the individual components and help you decide which tasks you want to do and what you expect your VA to do. Don't worry. Any task that is not your jam can be added to your hand-off list.

Breaking Down Your Boulders

Breaking down big tasks into their smallest steps is not a skill everyone has. Lucky for you it's my Zone of Genius and I'm going to share with you how I do this.

This process came to me backwards. I read the book, Tiny Habits by BJ Fogg, who discussed going super small to reach goals. When I read the book, I envisioned little pebbles that were holding back a huge boulder. If I could clear the pebbles, the boulder would eventually have no barrier and start rolling down the hill. Essentially, if I could declutter the things that blocked my goals, I'd get the momentum I needed to cross the finish line.

So if a goal is like a boulder, let's start with breaking that big rock into smaller chunks!

Picture this:

ROCKS - are the milestones we need to reach. Those are the checkpoints along the way that let us know we're making progress on our journey.

STONES - are the multi-action projects that get us to those milestones.

PEBBLES - are the individual tasks that make up projects.

SAND - the behaviors that become habits to create lasting change.

Not everyone looks at the little things that lead to big wins. Too often we're so focused on the big prize or the end zone that we discount all the little accomplishments along the way. In reality, these little wins done on a daily, weekly or monthly basis help us reach our destination much faster. The smaller you go means the easier it is to stay motivated and check things off your list. It seems counterintuitive but going small is the fastest way to reach your goal!

How do you do that?

Looking at your brain dump or goals list, identify your top three things to work on.

📢 ← Take Action

Using the **Breaking Down Goals** handout on the Resources webpage or a blank sheet of paper go through this 5-step process for each to crush that boulder into grains of sand.

Step One- Clarify Your Boulder

No one wakes up one day deciding to write a book or run a marathon and achieves it in one day. It takes hours spent at the computer pouring words onto a page or miles of training to cross the finish line.

Goals can be:

- Broad ideas like being more productive, getting healthy, being more organized.

- How we want to feel like more accomplished, stronger, more comfortable in our clothes, a sense of ease in our space.

- Specific outcomes like writing a book, creating a workshop, publishing your website.

When considering your goal(s), ask yourself the following questions to gain clarity: What is the goal? Is it a broad idea or a specific outcome or a mix of the two? What would it look like to achieve that goal and who do you need to become to make it happen? Is it a multi-step goal?

Clarify your goal(s). Include all the details you can think of.

Step Two- Smash the Boulder into Rocks

Imagine taking a sledgehammer to your boulder and breaking that too-big-to-climb mountain into smaller and more scalable Rocks.

Rocks are the incremental milestones along the journey to your goal that you need to reach. They are not the finish line. They are just mile markers reminding you that you ARE making progress like writing the outline for a book or finishing a 5K.

For each of your goals, envision the milestones and the rocks you need to smash for each and write them down. Be as specific as possible.

When I sat down to do this exercise when starting my podcast, the milestones I wrote down were outline and record Season 1, launch Podcast and market podcast.

Step Three- Crush Those Rocks into Stones

Milestones are made up of multi-step projects that have a beginning, middle and end. As you cross these off your list, you're moving further down the path to reaching your goal. These Stones roll easier but still take some effort. They are made of multiple smaller tasks that build on each other.

Writing a book is made up of projects like researching the topic, creating an outline, and writing the chapters. To go from the couch to running a marathon requires you first to walk, jog to build your stamina, and finally run.

Sometimes items that seem like they will be a single task surprise you. When you start to work on them, you discover they are made up of multiple steps.

When I looked at my first milestone to outline and record Season 1 of my podcast, my stones were to invite my friends to be co-hosts, brainstorm topics, and schedule recording sessions.

What steps do you need to take toward your goals?

What stones do you need to crush to reach your milestones?

Write down specific tasks.

Step Four- From Stones to Pebbles

Pebbles are single-action tasks. Once they are done, they're done! These are easy little wins that create momentum and energy to keep going like writing a chapter or walking around your neighborhood.

What individual, single-action tasks, or Pebbles make up your projects? Write them down. Be as specific as possible.

When looking at the single action pebbles, I sent individual emails to (3) friends, took the brainstorm list and wrote topic discussion points, scheduled recording sessions and led the podcast conversation. It all starts with clearing that first pebble. If I hadn't asked my co-hosts to join me, I probably wouldn't have gone through with the podcast.

People underestimate the freedom of clearing the blocks to a big task one small step at a time. It may feel like those single action tasks don't get you very far but small is mighty. The more pebbles you complete or hand off means the more momentum you create to then move on and smash stones, crush rocks and finally defeat the boulder or reach the big picture. Going small can be life-changing.

Step Five- Tiny Grains of Sand to Create Lasting Change

Many times our goals are not one-and-done. If we're not careful, those pebbles compound back to boulders. Grains of Sand are regular habits that keep those boulders from returning like going for a daily morning walk or meeting a friend for a weekly writing session.

What Grains of Sand do you need to create?

What daily, weekly, or monthly habit will help you to stay on track? Write them down. Be as specific as possible.

For the podcast, the grains of sand are showing up for recording sessions, listening to edited episodes, reviewing show notes, scheduling social media posts for air dates and sharing with people where to find it.

In business, your grains of sand could be: a daily inbox declutter, taking a moment each morning to write down three tasks to accomplish, and keeping an ongoing list of items to discuss with your VA at your next meeting.

Many of us have families, lives, and businesses. They all come with demands on our time, energy and resources. Grains of sand are often little pauses that allow us to create more room for the Pebbles, Stones and Rocks. They can be daily, weekly and monthly reminders to check in on what we said was important and a time to focus on those priorities.

Some goals only become manifested if we create a habit. If you want to be more organized, spending five minutes a day decluttering (papers, email, or calendar demands) will eventually lead to a clean to-be-filed folder, empty inbox or white space to dream bigger dreams.

Transform Your Brain Dump into a List

Now that you've broken down your goals, procrastinations and tolerations into single-action tasks, add them to your (probably very full) brain dump list. It's time to batch your tasks. Why? Because pairing tasks that go together like making calls or creating several graphics in one sitting makes it easier to get into a rhythm and flow. Batching items creates more ease.

Take Action

Using the **Categorize Your Lists** handout from the Resources webpage, work through your lists to pair and deduplicate items that overlap or are worded differently but essentially mean the same thing. Combine similar tasks under categories. Looking at your list, can you batch like items into broad, macro-level, umbrella-like categories? Can you see a pattern emerge?

Here are some examples of categories:

- Business, Personal, Health, Hobby, Family, Goals.
- Love It/Like It/Hate It List.
- Items that are in your Zone of Genius, Zone of Excellence, Zone of Competence and Zone of Incompetence (as outlined in The Big Leap by Gay Hendricks).

Pay particular attention to items on the list that you know already energetically drain you or you keep putting off because you just don't want to do them. Make this a separate HAND-OFF category. Just like that, your list is starting.

If having several categories is too overwhelming, start with two simple headers like **Business** and **Personal.** You should be able to look at any item on your list and know if it's one or the other.

Then sort those further. For example, under Business, you can create a **Business - Running** heading for tasks like invoicing, bill paying, and scheduling and a **Business - Growth** heading for tasks like social media, newsletters and networking. **Personal** could be split into **Family, Personal Growth**, and **Self-care.** Keep narrowing down the categories as you go.

Don't worry! If you haven't done an exercise like this before, let your brain marinate. As we go forward, your inner organizer may emerge and the concept will reveal itself for you.

Once you have your categories, it's time to drill down to reality and see where the freedom and relief can come from!

Everyone has their own unique talents. If you know yours, as you go through your list, you'll spot the items that you can't wait to tackle and those you'll push off for as long as possible. Relief is coming. I promise because ...not every task on your list needs to be done by you.

HAVE vs. "Have-tos"

There are two kinds of "Have-tos":

The "have to" items you feel like only you are qualified to handle (like scheduling client calls or sending out business contracts) but if systems were put in place and a little training given, someone else could do it.

The HAVE to items are those that no one else can do for you like meeting with clients or delivering a webinar.

With that in mind, sort your newly categorized list using The **4D Method**. Mark items: DO, DELEGATE, DELETE or DELAY.

DO tasks are those that you're excited about, can't wait to do, or you *HAVE* to do.

DELEGATE tasks are those that drain you, you keep putting off, or could easily be handed off to someone else.

DELETE like tossing that old shirt you never wear, it's okay to delete items that once seemed important to accomplish but no longer serve you or your business.

DELAY tasks can wait. Other items might have higher priority and these will get done when time, energy and resources allow. For example: maybe now isn't the right time to write that book you have in mind but eventually, you'll get to it.

After labeling your tasks, shift them onto their own lists or print **The D List** worksheet in the Resource webpage. Like taking the bag of trash to the curb, get the Delete items off your list and out of your head. You don't need to transfer these tasks.

Now you can more easily see what you HAVE to do, what you can take off your mind and what to hand off.

Prioritize your lists

Congratulations!! You did it! You now have your Hand-off List!

TA-Do to TA-DONE

So often a client will complain about how little they got done in a day but they were "super busy." I can relate. Have you ever been sideswiped by a shiny object, an emergency call, or just a feeling of blah that kept you from doing the items on your to-do list? However, by the end of the day, you know you did stuff.

A bonus category that I love sharing is creating a TA-Done list. A TA-Done list celebrates the doing of the tasks that never make it onto any list but you did them. To make myself feel more productive because I was actually accomplishing stuff, I write completed tasks onto my TA-done list just to cross them off and remind myself of all the things I've accomplished and where my energy was spent.

Celebration is key to motivation. Any way you can celebrate is a good thing so HIGH FIVE for tasks that get done without realization.

Woohoo! High-five! You earned it!

Before you go rushing into a discovery call with a VA ready to shove your list onto their plate, there are a few more steps.

Let's look at your priorities... Without priorities, it's hard to know what to do first.

Establishing your priorities creates a hierarchy of what you need to do first and where any new to-do items will fall on your existing lists.

When picking your priorities, take into account everything that is happening in your life. None of us live or work in a vacuum. It's all connected for us. In some instances, as much as we'd like to focus solely on our own goals, our priorities for a week or a month may have nothing to do with them. A family emergency or situation outside of our control can take over our time and focus, pushing our goals to the back burner.

From your Do and Delegate lists, pick three items each to make a priority. It can be larger tasks on your to-do list or have nothing to do with work like spending more time with family and friends. They can be specific or broad but NO MORE THAN three. Any more than that becomes a list.

Once you set them, write your two lists on their own 3x5 index cards or Post-its and put them where you'll see them daily.

Whenever you feel stuck, look at your "Do" priorities and ask yourself if what you're doing or not doing is in line with your priorities. If not, what can you be doing instead?

Knowing your "Delegate" priorities will help you determine what kind of VA support you need. We'll explore the different kinds of support in the next chapter. Keep your hand-off list and Delegate priorities handy because you'll need them.

Recap: Key Points

- Define Your Hand-Off List: Questions to consider: What do you enjoy most? What drains your energy? What tasks can someone else do better or faster?

- Conduct a Brain Dump: Clear your mind by writing down every idea, task, or goal no matter how big or small. Include procrastinations (tasks you delay) and tolerations (minor annoyances you endure) to identify areas needing attention.

- Break Down Larger Goals using the Boulder-to-Sand method:

  Boulders: Overarching goals.
  Rocks: Milestones to achieve the goal.
  Stones: Multi-step projects.
  Pebbles: Individual tasks.
  Sand: Habits to maintain the progress.

- Organize and Categorize Tasks: Group tasks into broad categories like business, personal, or specific types (e.g., social media, admin tasks).

- Use The 4D Method to sort tasks into Do, Delegate, Delete, or Delay.

- Set clear priorities for your tasks to focus on what is most important.

Journal Prompts

☺ What tasks or projects feel most aligned with my passions and what is stopping me from prioritizing them?

☺ What am I constantly avoiding or tolerating and how does it impact my energy or progress?

☺ What level of comfort do I need to create in order to let someone help me with my Delegate tasks?

Chapter Three

Not All VAs Are the Same

One of the greatest misconceptions about the VA industry is that all virtual assistants are the same. VAs offer a wide range of services and are highly skilled. They provide administrative, operations, and (sometimes) personal support in a broad way. They may offer specialized skills like bookkeeping, web design or marketing, but they are not professional in those areas.

Since I became a virtual assistant in 2005, the industry has boomed and the term Virtual Assistant (VA) is used interchangeably for all kinds of assistants from the AI customer service chatbot on websites to highly specialized executive level assistants.

By definition, a virtual assistant (VA) handles administrative items that can be done virtually using phone, email and web-based technology. A VA is a business owner and not an employee. As a contractor, they are responsible for paying their own bills and overhead. The client only pays for hours worked.

This means a VA can complete certain aspects of multiple professions like invoicing, website updates and content planning for social media. However, they are not likely certified bookkeepers, web designers or marketing strategy specialists.

Also, not everyone who can do administrative tasks is a virtual assistant. Your friend's daughter who likes to do data entry as a side job is not a VA. A superfan who has been to all your workshops and "wants to help" may not be the right fit to manage your social media.

Many types of support are included under the term Virtual Assistant. By my definition, not all of those listed are actual virtual assistants.

The Five Kinds of Support Types:

1. Specialists

If your task list requires specialized expertise, it's better to hire a specialist like a bookkeeper, videographer, graphic designer, web designer, or marketing specialist.

2. Personal Assistants, Housekeepers and Nannies

If the majority of your hand-off tasks need to be done in real life like grocery shopping, going to the dry cleaner, picking up your kids and handling your mail, you'll want to explore hiring a personal assistant, housekeeper or nanny.

3. Employees

Sometimes an employee is what you need. This is especially true if you require a full-time in-house person or you don't like having your support person be out of sight.

However, if your list can be done virtually and falls into a broad administrative scope of work, a virtual assistant is what you're looking for.

In my experience, I've identified two kinds of VAs: Doers and Collaborators. All are equally wonderful and offer varying levels of expertise and support. Where they differ is the way they support clients.

4. Doer VAs

Doer VAs are detail and task oriented. While Collaborators will tell you how they can help, Doers will request, "Tell me what you want me to do". Doers require more upfront work and guidance from the client. They keep their focus on the task at hand without offering much collaboration. They do better with tasks that are easily duplicated and have clear processes and instructions.

5. Collaborator VAs

Collaborator VAs look at the whole picture of your business goals and needs. They look at each task with an eye for its role in the long-term. Collaborators are solution-oriented and tend to be able to step into a business and offer suggestions for improvement. Some clients may start out with a Collaborator VA to create their processes and procedures so they can then hand off the daily work to a Doer VA. Sometimes they're called an Online Business Manager (OBM) who is like a Chief of Staff and can help run a team of VAs or specialists.

5a. Doers leaning into Collaborators

Sometimes you'll find someone straddling the fence. I call them Doers leaning into Collaborators. These are Doers with some years of client experience. They know how some tasks work and can offer suggestions to streamline the process to save time or money. They offer their experience to collaborate while still preferring to comple the tasks at hand.

What do you need?

It comes down to the intention and preference of the entrepreneur. Are you simply handing over a to-do list with ready made instructions or are you looking for someone to help streamline your business to run its best?

One thing to know is that Virtual Assistants were never meant to be a cheap alternative to hiring an employee. While there are low cost overseas VAs who are great, most Canada and US based virtual assistants will charge between $40-100 per hour depending on their skills and experience. You get what you pay for.

Problems arise when a business owner chooses a support person on the basis of cost rather than the type of support they actually need. When figuring out what kind of support you need, consider the following:

- Where are you in the process of creating your business?
- What kind of leadership/manager style are you?
- Do you have a clear picture of what you want your VA to do? Can you clearly explain it?
- Do you have detailed processes and procedures or do you need support to create them?
- Do you need someone long term or for a one-off project?

It's also perfectly acceptable for a client to start with one type of support to clear items off their hand-off list in order to set themselves up for other kinds of support. For example, if your priority is to get your website up and running, you may look for a web design specialist versus finding a VA whose skills are better at maintaining a completed site or hiring a Marketing Specialist to help you create a marketing plan and then hiring a VA to help you implement it.

Take Action

How do you figure out what support flow you need?

Using the **Delegate Priorities** handout in the Resources webpage to help, take your Delegate items and prioritize the tasks in the order you want someone to complete them. _Using the codes below, next to each task, mark what kind of support person would do the best job:_

- Specialist (S)
- Personal Assistant (PA)
- Collaborator VA (CVA)
- Doer VA (DVA)
- Employee (E)

Add up each code and list the support person type(s) that makes the most sense to complete your priority projects first. If you need to work with more than one type, note which one you will work with first or if they will collaborate together.

For example, let's say you have a priority project to create a video series on YouTube. Listing the tasks, you need to work with a video editor (specialist) who also creates intro/outro pieces as well as a virtual assistant who can upload the videos to YouTube and create promotional graphics to share with social media.

Depending on your budget and leadership style, you may work with the video editor first to complete the project and then hire the VA to do the rest. In the alternative, your VA might work on their piece while your video editor gets their project done or you hand the project off to your VA to work with the video editor while you give approval or edits as needed.

Run the remaining items on your hand-off list through your priority filter. Ask yourself these questions:

- Are any of the tasks items that will move me forward on my goals?
- Are any of the tasks standing in the way of moving my goals forward?
- Are any of the tasks time sensitive or have a deadline?
- Does it make sense to do your priorities in the order you established them or would it make more sense to clear more low level tasks to get those TA-Done?

Priority projects may be knocking loudly to be accomplished but while VAs are highly skilled and knowledgeable about most things, tasks still take time. For example, priority tasks can be:

- Adding social media to your marketing
- Starting a newsletter

- Writing a book to establish your professional credibility.

If you're not consistently invoicing clients or often have scheduling conflicts, having a VA get those sorted out may be a higher priority than implementing a social media strategy.

If you haven't finished your website, it might be better to hold off sending out a newsletter. If you have no marketing presence, selling your book will be harder.

Having a budget in mind will help you and your VA decide how much time you can comfortably afford and what order makes sense to accomplish your task list.

You might be saying everything on the list is important and while that might be true, your wallet might disagree with the amount of hours it would take to do everything right away. Using our video series project example, this may be a priority goal but is it the best use of your time and resources if you are still doing tasks that steal time and energy? In looking at your list with your budget in mind, it may be better to delay this task until you create more space and resources to focus on it.

If you shift your priority task list, does the support person you noted still work for the rest of your list or do you need a different type?

Having an outline of your prioritized hand-off list will help you build a stronger foundation under your business and convey your vision when talking with potential helpers.

Different Types of Virtual Assistants

Within Doer and Collaborator VAs, you will find terms like solopreneurs, teams, Online Business Managers (OBMs) and agencies.

Let's define them.

Solopreneurs: Solopreneurs work independently with clients. They can be Doers or Collaborators. If a client needs a skill or service they don't do, they often refer the client to work with a different VA on those tasks. The solopreneur does not act as the middleman. They may coordinate some of the work but payment, contracts and working relationships are between the client and the other VA.

Teams: Teams often have a main center point of contact who works with the client and then hands off the tasks to team members. My colleague, Bree BV with BeeVee Pro, runs a team in Canada. Her team's approach to working with clients usually involves assigning at least two team members to collaborate on each client's project including the team lead and another member. The benefit of this setup is the collaboration that happens behind the scenes to ensure multiple perspectives and ideas contribute to strategies and their implementation. In situations where unexpected events occur such as illness, family emergencies, or vacations, having multiple team members involved ensures continuity. Another team member is always available who understands the project and maintains a connection with the client. Depending on the project's scope, there may be up to three or four team members involved depending on their specific skill set and interests.

Other teams may run differently with a client being handed off to a specific team member or the work being divided between VAs.

Online Business Managers (OBMs): tend to operate like a Chief of Staff. They are not necessarily the doer of the work. They are the manager of the people that do the doing. They come into a client's business if the client is already working with multiple VAs and needs someone to manage the team they built or they bring their own team to support a client. OBMs are helpful if a client needs support to manage communication with non-connected VAs.

Agencies: There are two different styles that I want to call attention to: the Traditional Agency and a new up and coming Boutique Agency.

> **A Traditional Agency** is not the same as a team. There are generally a couple of different models for how work is handled. One model involves the client submitting work to be completed which then goes into a queue. Team members in the agency work on tasks based on their availability and return it once completed.
>
> The other model involves assigning a team member to a client from the agency. This assignment could be for a shorter duration, such as a week or a month, after which it rotates to another team member based on the agency's needs. This is less personal and more transactional.
>
> **A Boutique Agency** on the other hand does run like a team. There is more relationship building between the agency point of contact and the client while still having a team of

VAs who specialize in various tasks doing the work. These tend to be smaller agencies who offer more of a personal touch. Behind the scenes they work together more like a team than as simple subcontractors doing tasks.

Since my intention with this book is to showcase the business to business relationship between the client and the VA, I feel I should add a warning here. While solopreneurs, teams and OBMs are VA businesses working with client businesses, a client's relationship with an agency is with the agency and not necessarily with the "VAs" doing the work. The VAs at an agency are not usually part of the business relationship. They get assigned to the people they work for and what tasks they do.

This is still ok as long as the client knows this is the type of relationship they are getting. Some businesses do very well with this type of relationship (especially those that are task focused rather than relationship focused). However, if you're looking to form a bond with your VA, this is not the way to go.

I have found agencies are a love it or hate it experience so do some research before signing with any agency. Make sure its style of work matches yours and that you feel comfortable with the terms. Many agencies have higher retainers or blocks of hours but they tend to offer a more all-in-one solution for a wide range of services.

If you don't know what business model a potential VA or agency is utilizing, ask. Please note that Doer and Collaborator VAs and Traditional and Boutique Agencies are my terms.

Overseas VAs

Many people ask about the pros and cons of hiring from a domestic or overseas VA. Overseas VAs have become synonymous with low-cost or the "$5 VA". Due to the difference in the cost of living in parts of the world, this can be true. Low cost does not always equate to low quality. One of my VAs runs a team from the Philippines and produces the most gorgeous graphics and videos for me. For task-oriented and repetitive work, they can be a great fit.

While the term overseas in the US is usually associated with VAs from the Philippines, VAs are found worldwide in places like India, Latin America, Africa, Europe, Canada and beyond. It can also depend on where you're located. For example, for business owners living in the United States, any VA not in North America is overseas. Since all VA work is virtual, some US based VAs may live in other countries and technically be considered overseas VAs.

There are some things to consider before hiring a VA outside of your country.

Time differences: A benefit is this can extend your workday without requiring you to work longer hours. You can hand off work at the end of your day and by the time you return to work, the tasks are done. A con is valuable time can be lost when questions come up.

Language barriers: Language barriers can be a challenge but when you provide clear instructions, tasks can be performed well. Be considerate when using slang. Those of us who speak English as a first language can sometimes take shortcuts with words or use idioms which can confuse non-native speakers.

For example, a client once asked for "edgy" pictures which the VA interpreted as pictures of edges (like cliffs and tables).

The difference between working with a team, OBM, agency and overseas VA depends on how much control and collaboration you want to have with the VA doing your work. If you're okay with a task-oriented Doer and have easily repeated tasks with clear processes and procedures, then an overseas VA or agency might work well for you.

Take your budget and task needs into account. While the price point can be really good, many agencies usually start with a 20-hours-a-month retainer. If you're just starting out, you may not have 20 hours a month of work to hand off so you could be paying for time not used. You may have a project that should take a short amount of time but will take longer because many hands are touching it. Mistakes can happen because VAs are human. In all instances, there should be a quality check between the task doer and the client. As a client, you are responsible to check all work done and communicate changes and approval. Note that the back and forth adds time and time equates to money. We'll get into pricing structures and budgets in the next chapter.

Remember that the VA industry is highly collaborative. If a VA doesn't do the work, they can get it done by asking a friend or colleague. So whether you work with a solopreneur, team, agency or overseas VA, focus on finding the right fit. When you do, you'll discover some of those items you thought you HAD to do may shift to your delegate list.

As time goes on and your time and energy free up, you'll find your well of creativity fills. Soon you're ready to focus on those

Delayed items and even new ideas you can't yet imagine and that's where freedom, ease and growth start to happen. Having the right VA on your team allows you to shift your focus back to the reasons you got into business in the first place and your business will grow!

Recap: Key Points

- **Matching Support to Needs**
Different tasks require different types of support such as Specialists, Personal Assistants, VAs, or full-time employees. Entrepreneurs should align their task list and priorities with the type of support needed to ensure the best fit for their business goals.

- **Types of Virtual Assistants (VAs):**
The concept of Virtual Assistance is broad.

  - **Teams:** Teams have a central point of contact and multiple members collaborating on client projects to ensure continuity and diverse perspectives.

  - **Online Business Managers (OBMs):** These VAs manage other VAs and handle communication and operate like a Chief of Staff.

- **Agency Models:**
    Queue-Based: Work is submitted and placed in a queue. Available team members pick up tasks and complete them based on their capacity.

    Assigned Team Members: A specific team member is assigned to a client for a shorter duration and rotates based on the agency's needs.

- **Independent VAs**
    VAs can be categorized as Doers (task-oriented and focused on detailed instructions) and Collaborators (strategic and focused on long-term goals and business improvement).

    Solopreneurs: Independent VAs who can be Doers or Collaborators. They refer clients to other VAs for skills they don't possess without acting as middlemen.

    Domestic VAs: Located within the same country or region as the client, they offer cultural and time zone compatibility.

    Overseas VAs: Typically associated with lower costs due to different living standards. Effective for repetitive tasks but requires clear communication to overcome language barriers.

- **Cost and Value:**
Hiring a VA is not a cheaper alternative to an employee but a strategic choice to delegate tasks efficiently. Canada and U.S.-based VAs typically charge $40-$100 per hour depending on their skills and experience and the right VA brings significant value to the business.

Journal Prompts

☺ Reviewing my hand-off list, which type of VA feels most aligned with my needs and work style right now?

☺ How might my support needs evolve over time and how can I remain flexible in adapting to those changes?

☺ As I went through my list, did my priorities shift? How?

Chapter Four

Establish Your Budget

You might be wondering why we spent so much time guiding you to your perfect VA in Chapter Three with bare mentions of your budget. I'll tell you. It is because I've seen so many people hire a VA based on the cheapest rate they can find rather than finding someone who is actually going to help lighten their load and propel their business forward. Remember that not all VAs are the same and sometimes you get what you pay for.

Cost is the number one determining factor I've heard potential clients share when it comes to finding a virtual assistant. If your budget is small, how do you pay for the right fit? So many have started their VA/client journey with the least expensive option only to discover it was the wrong fit. As you'll learn in this chapter, you can find the right VA for your business needs at any budget.

First, many clients don't consider their budget until they start working with someone and feel the pinch. For just a moment, let's ignore the types of VAs and only look at your fiscal capabilities.

- How much money are you comfortable spending per month for support?

- Do you have recurring monthly income to help support the costs of hiring someone?

- Can you view hiring someone as an investment in your business or is it simply an expense?

- How much money are you losing in your business because you are unable to focus on it?

When it comes to your budget, I always say let your budget guide you but don't let it rule you. There is support available for all budgets.

You could hire a strategist to create a plan.

You could hire a VA on a project basis to reduce pain points to a manageable level like setting up automations, creating an SOP, or drafting a template for your newsletter.

You could start with a smaller number of hours to get into a flow to start delegating tasks and clearing small things off your plate.

This may mean managing expectations and elongating your timeline for completing some projects but working with a VA can be done. There is wiggle room in determining how much you can spend, how many hours that looks like, and what kind of VA you can utilize that pool of money for. It doesn't serve you or your budding relationship with your VA to start where you are financially uncomfortable or at a level that is unsustainable. If it helps to start on the smaller end, do it. If $200-300 a month is all you can spend, *that* is your budget.

Looking at your finances, choose a dollar range you are comfortable spending every month. It's important to be realistic with this number. Write this number down. We'll need it later in the chapter.

In the last chapter, we discussed the different types of VAs. When you were looking at your hand-off and delegate list, what type of VA did you decide would be the best fit for you? The type of VA you've chosen will help you determine how many hours your budget will support. Since different VAs charge different rates, if you have a $300 budget, you could get 10 hours at $30 an hour or five hours at $60 an hour.

Remember that a VA was never meant to be a low-cost option for an employee. Employees get paid by the employer. The employer factors in the cost of overhead, taxes, time off, and benefits when calculating what they will pay hourly.

An employee gets paid whether they're at their desk, talking to a co-worker or wandering the halls. A VA is their own business and they handle their overhead, taxes, and everything. A VA only charges for the time they actually spend working on your project, call or training.

Many times when calculating the number of hours needed, a client thinks about how long it takes for them to do the work. A VA's hour is different from yours.

Early in my career when email marketing was in its infancy, I met someone who became a client at a Constant Contact training. She was doing marketing for a small spa and looking to incorporate email marketing into their strategy. I was a business partner and trainer for Constant Contact and gave her my card. She called me when she had hit her limit with trying to figure out how to create the spa's first newsletter. She had exceeded her paid retainer hours without completing the task. After 30 minutes of working on it together, we hit send. It cost her way more time and money to do the work than to hire me to do it for her.

If a project takes you a long time and you hire someone who specializes in that task, it's going to take them less time. Since they track their time when they start and stop working on the project, they can more easily show how long the project actually takes. Unlike when you go through your day doing your work, a VA doesn't add time spent on interruptions, calls, breaks, or other client work to your totals. A two hour project could be split over a whole month in short 15-minute increments.

Beginning Costs

In the beginning of working together, it will take your VA extra time to get to know your business, work and brand. The first few months of the VA/Client relationship is a learning period for both of you. It may feel like you're spending more time and money. View this time as an investment. The more your VA gets to know you in the beginning means the less handholding and micromanaging you'll have to do later. Your VA will be able to take on new tasks without extra guidance from you which will save you time and money later.

Since not all VAs are the same, knowing what kind of VA you need and how much they usually charge will help connect your budget to the right type of package.

As of this writing in 2025, the average rates in U.S. Dollars are:

- Doer: *$20-40 per hour* .
- Doer leaning to Collaborator: *$40-65 per hour.*
- Collaborator: *$50-100+per hour.*
- Online Business Manager: *$75-150+ per hour.*
- Specialist: *$75-150+ per hour.*

When you're thinking about budget and the amount of hours that you need, factor extra hours for getting to know each other.

Employees usually get a 90-day probationary window to learn their job and the company culture.

Try working with a VA for at least that amount of time. Of course, if it's not working out, you don't have to stick it out.

You should understand that even the most highly skilled VA can't just walk into a business and know everything.

There are different payment options. Knowing these will help you determine what you're most comfortable with and find a VA who fits the bill (no pun intended).

- **Hourly or Pay-As-You-Go (PAYG):** time worked is tracked and billed by the hour, usually in 15-minute increments and invoiced to the client at the end of the month.

- **Retainer:** a pre-paid package, usually starting at 10-20 hours per month and invoiced up front. Any unused hours do not usually rollover to the next month. A good option if you're sure you'll use the number of hours every month.

- **Debit Card:** a pre-paid package of hours, usually 10-20 hours. Unlike a retainer, these hours do rollover and have an expiration date of 3-12 months.

- **Projects:** a quoted rate for specific deliverables.

- **Day Rate/VIP Day:** a set package of hours used in one day rather than spread throughout a month. Good for one off projects that don't require ongoing support.

Hourly, Retainer and Debit Card time is usually tracked in 15-minute increments. The difference is when they are invoiced and whether the hours roll over or not. Hourly rates tend to be higher than discounted package rates. The more hours you purchase means the lower the price per hour. Deciding on the right billing plan is as unique as your business needs.

Do you need only one-time work for a specific project?
Go with Projects.

Unsure of how many hours you need?
Start with Hourly/ PAYG until you know what you will use.

Need a block of focused time?
A Day Rate/VIP Day option is great to get stuff done in a short period of time.

Are you looking to build a relationship with a reliable professional?
Go with a Retainer or Debit Card. It will encourage you to utilize your support.

The minimum package for teams and agencies may be higher than solopreneurs. Some may offer month-to-month or hourly to start in order to get a sense of what the client needs while others require a long-term contract. These standards should be communicated during the interview process and if the VA doesn't bring up their offerings, ask for details.

A billing option is not set in stone. Some VAs have their preferred ways to charge but if you feel more comfortable starting with hourly rates until you know how many hours you would use in a package, do it. If you prefer to pay for a retainer to keep you accountable to handing off tasks, that works too.

There is no right or wrong way to go and you can adjust as you need.

≡ Take Action

Figure Out Your Budget
It's time to crunch some numbers.

In the Resources webpage, I've added my **Figure Out Your Budget** worksheet to help.

First, look at your finances and jot down the minimum and maximum monthly dollar amount you are comfortable spending or pull out the number you wrote down at the beginning of the chapter.

Next, consider what kind of virtual assistant support you think you need:
Doer VA ($20-40 per hour)
Collaborator VA ($50-100 per hour)
Online Business Managers ($75-100+ per hour)

Divide your minimum and maximum monthly budget by the average hourly rate range for your preferred support type.

Now consider how many hours you think you'll need per month. Where does that fall in the hourly range?

For example, let's say your budget is $300-500 a month and you need a Collaborator VA. If the minimum hourly rate is $50 and the maximum hourly rate is $100, that means at minimum you get (3-5) hours a month or max (6-10) hours a month. If your needs are 5-10 hours a month, you need to look for a $ 50-an-hour VA to get your tasks done.

A word of caution: If you're starting with a 10-20 hours a month retainer, that many hours may not feel like a lot considering the number of tasks on your hand-off list but until you know how much time you need, it may be too much. Unless you are sure that you need that level of time every month, start with a smaller retainer or package.

Make sure to keep the lines of communication open with your VA. Sometimes a project takes longer than expected or delays in deadlines can elongate the number of hours used.

For instance, have you ever received an email only to get a second "oops" email with a fix? Have you ever added an extra speaker to a summit at the last minute forgetting about the corresponding cascade of tasks?

These tasks and more can't always get factored in ahead of time but time is money. Last minute additions and changes often have hidden tasks that take more time than a client realizes. This is part of running a business. We can't anticipate every "what-if" but we can rise to the occasion when unexpected situations come up.

There are a lot of ways a VA can save you money and not just by taking tasks off your plate. Experienced VAs use what they know from working with multiple clients to reduce the amount of time spent on a task. While this may sound counterintuitive since time spent equals dollars charged, VAs are task oriented. We don't want to spend longer on something when completing it means more time to work on other equally important tasks for clients. Personally, I love working on the tasks that help drive my client's goals forward.

If this is your first time working with a VA or an assistant, there could be a learning curve for how you work with someone else. You can grow with your VA and a VA can grow with you. As time goes on and they gain more skills and experience, expect their rates to increase.

Letting your VA help guide you may take some getting used to but it will be worth it in the long run. My colleague Bree BV with BeeVeePro put together a handy resource for ways to save with a VA. Her guidebook **"Save Time & Increase Productivity: Working with a Virtual Assistant,"** is in the Resources webpage. Here are some quick tips:

- **Clear communication:** when handing off projects be sure to give clear deadlines, key dates, workflows with links to templates, and priorities of tasks. Ask for weekly or mid-point progress reports to keep your budget in mind. It sucks when an invoice is much higher than expected due to miscommunication.

- **Keep everything in one place:** like where you communicate with each other (text, email, Slack, or a CRM) don't bounce around platforms making it hard to find answers to questions and put documents or images in one location.

- **Leverage technology:** using cloud-based and collaborative programs like Google Drive Suite can keep all comments and to-dos in one document and reduce the time going back and forth. Utilizing videos like a 5-minute Loom to show a process can reduce the need for lengthy calls.

- **Batch work:** tasks like social media, graphic creation, and events are made up of lots of little tasks. Giving all the needed information means the VA can easily go from task to task and shorten the amount of time getting into and out of the flow. Seeing all the work at the same time can often result in catching errors.

Ask your VA for ways to help you save. But before you can, you first need to find a VA.

No matter what your budget is, start small and build trust. What is your biggest pain point? What task will make the most impact? Is it starting a social media plan or getting out a newsletter?

This first project may not take up your whole budget for the month but if it's a really big project or your budget is on the smaller side, it may take a few months to complete. Either way, getting it done will free up time and energy and show you how good it feels to work with the VA.

Whew! Thinking about financials is not my favorite thing. If looking at money is hard for you too, *Congratulations! You did it!*

We all get into business to make money but money is a fickle mistress. If you don't pay attention to her, she'll leave. It's not always fun to consider the money side of our business but it's part of wearing the business owner hat. High-five to you for doing the hard thing and figuring out your budget!

With your budget and type of VA top of mind, what qualities does this person need to have? We'll talk about that in the next chapter.

Recap: Key Points

Let your budget guide you; don't let it rule you.

- Cost is often the main deciding factor for hiring a virtual assistant (VA) but selecting the least expensive option may not yield the best fit. Quality and value are important to consider alongside budget.

- Assess how much you can realistically and comfortably spend each month on VA support. View the expense as an investment in your business rather than just a cost.

- VA rates vary by expertise and currency.

- Payment options include hourly, retainers, projects, day rates, or debit card packages.

- A VA's work hour differs from an employee's as it focuses solely on productive tasks which avoids inefficiencies like interruptions or breaks.

- Begin with a manageable number of hours and smaller tasks. This approach helps establish trust and ensures financial sustainability as the relationship develops.

- The initial months with a VA may require more time and effort as they learn your business. This upfront investment leads to greater efficiency and independence later.

Journal Prompts

What is a realistic monthly budget for VA support that aligns with my financial comfort and business goals?

Can I view hiring a VA as an investment rather than a cost?

Which tasks are costing me the most?

Chapter Five

Qualities Beyond the Task List

The risk I see most potential clients take isn't hiring a VA. It is going into the process blind on how to find the right fit. Maybe it's just me but I believe that if you're going to take the risk of letting somebody into your business, you should do the hard work to discover what it is you actually need in the person.

If your business is your baby, you wouldn't entrust it to just anyone. You would want to find someone responsible who you can rely on. This chapter is about figuring out what you need to learn about the person to answer the gut vibe check.

Finding the right help is a lot like dating. On paper or the internet, an entrepreneur is putting his/her best face forward like an online dating profile. It's easy to swipe right or left when you see an About Me or Services page and you do or don't like what it says.

However, you wouldn't marry someone just because they list all the same likes as you. You would want to get to know the person behind the profile. This is why dating a potential VA is so important. Don't just date one either. Interview a few people even if someone stands out right away.

My friend Jessica and I often held jobs that overlapped people we knew in the theater world. I remember having a conversation with her about two different stage managers we had both worked with. She liked one whom I did not get along with. All the qualities in him that made my skin prickle were the qualities she admired in him. While I loved the other boss, my friend couldn't stand him for the same reasons. Both stage managers were equally great but they had different personalities, ways of communicating, and overall vibe. Different people will connect with different qualities.

The same can be true when meeting with virtual assistants and especially those that come as referrals or who are already working with someone you know. Just because they get along doesn't mean you will and vice versa. When working in someone else's business, you're not always able to pick who you get to work with. However, this is your business and finding the right VA for you is in your hands.

We will discuss interviews in the next chapter. For now, let's get clear on the qualities you're looking for in your perfect partner beyond your task list. Once you have this list, you will be able to craft questions for the interview process to discover if the person you're talking to has them.

Over the years, many potential clients have come to me in trepidation because they had worked with a virtual assistant before and it didn't work out or they had heard so many horror stories that they were afraid to find someone because they were certain they would make the wrong choice.

I get it!

When coaches, programs, books, and time management experts simply say "hire a VA" but don't expand on what to look for, it's no wonder people are lost and confused. As we've learned so far, hiring a VA is not a one-size-fits-all endeavor.

The thing I love about being a virtual assistant is how different each one of us is and how that is a gift for clients. Although VAs can do the same kind of tasks and work in the same types of programs, we each have a unique voice, history, and viewpoint of the world which makes all the difference to the VA/Client relationship.

By now you have your hand-off list, know your budget, and probably have a good idea of what type of VA you're looking for but what do you need in the person other than the title?

Words of Wisdom
My mentor once told me, "We could learn something new every day and still not know everything". This is so true. Through our own interests or because of client needs, VAs tend to gain skills at a faster rate than we can update our websites and services offered page. This prompted the motto: "Ask, Always Ask."

Due to the myriad of ways someone comes to the industry, many VAs offer clients more skills than just administrative ones. I know many stay-at-home moms and military spouses who have started VA businesses after being "out of the workforce" for so long that they don't feel qualified for a J.O.B. or were unable to hold a steady position due to constant moving from one base to another or their kids' school schedules.

However, if you look at the skills they have acquired through the years of running and maintaining a family and supporting their spouse's career, running a client's business is relatively easy in comparison. Even if a VA is new to their business, they may have life experience that can be invaluable to clients.

For example, I worked with a newbie VA who had twenty years of experience in magazine editing, proofreading and content creation. She is a wiz for anyone who needs support with coming up with content and making it read professionally. Her lack of years as a business owner doesn't negate her years of experience doing the work. It enhances it.

VAs often take on the role of accountability partners, therapists, business coaches and collaborators for clients. We use our years of experience in life in many capacities beyond the services we offer to our clients. During a call, my client told me that he had planned to hire a business coach after we got our rhythm but he no longer felt the need to find someone because of the advice I gave him.

Lots of times clients are in such a state of overwhelm that they don't know what they need beyond help. That's okay. Start where you are and grow from there. Even having a basic idea of the qualities you're looking for can help you get started. If you start with someone who isn't the right fit for the long term, they may help get you to the place where you can take better stock of what will be a better fit later. Someone who may not initially have all the skills you're looking for may gain them as you grow together.

What are your quality preferences?
Creating a quality list isn't as hard as one might think. Having

even a vague idea of what you like and don't like in a person can go a long way in weeding out possibilities for initial conversations.

If a VA is a business partner, look back at previous bosses, coworkers and clients and decide what qualities you liked and didn't like.

- What did you like about working with them and what did you not?

- What qualities attract you to a person and what repels you?

Even if all the qualities you are looking for are there on paper, trust your gut. A vibe or a feeling can change your response from yes to no.

When you ask long standing married couples why they work so well together, most say good communication or that the other person fills in their gaps. Good communication is key to building a great working relationship between virtual assistants and their clients. It's not just about how you prefer to communicate (whether that is email, phone, or text). It's also about making sure both sides understand each other.

When my husband and I first moved in together, a lot of our fights centered around where the other wasn't "doing it right." I didn't use enough soap in the washing machine or hubby wouldn't put away the clean clothes. Hubby liked to cook but not do the dishes while I didn't get the counters clean enough. The list went on and on until one night we had a conversation where we aired all our grievances and compromised on each of us doing the tasks that mattered more to us than to the other or that we didn't want to do. Hubby took over washing and drying the laundry while I folded, hung up and put the clean clothes away. After dinner, I would wash the dishes and hubby would wipe down the counters. This division of labor is how most successful relationships manage.

When you're considering the qualities beyond your task list, *look at your gaps*:

- If you feel disorganized and forgetful, you may look for someone who is naturally organized who can help you create systems or send reminders.

- If there are aspects of your business that are falling through the cracks, who would be the best type of person to plug those leaks?

Other Factors To Consider

Communication Styles
Plenty of little quirks can come up in communication and especially if there is a big age gap or cultural difference between you and your VA. For example, some people might use all caps in their emails or add lots of exclamation points which can feel intense if you're not used to it. Others might prefer to talk things through over the phone if technology or writing everything down isn't their strong suit. Some people love to spend a little time chatting and building a connection while others just want quick no-frills updates. Some people want all the details while others prefer succinct, bullet point recaps. Language slang or idioms may not translate and need extra clarification.

Knowing your communication style and needs can make finding a way to meet in the middle easier and more enjoyable. Flexibility is very important because every relationship is different.

Do you need weekly calls to feel secure?

If you don't like checking email, is there another communication tool that you respond to better?

At first, you may need a bit more back-and-forth until trust is built and you've established a good routine. Over time, you can adjust how often you meet or how updates are shared to fit what works best for both of you. It may include creating a new communication channel just for this relationship. Even things like sending voice memos or finding creative ways to share ideas can help keep communication simple and effective.

It's not just everyday communication.

How do you communicate anger or disappointment when mistakes happen? No matter how good a VA is at their job, mistakes happen. How do you work through those mistakes? Can you handle mistakes with grace? Are you able to take responsibility for your part? Are you open to having the hard conversations and giving the benefit of the doubt or are you a one-and-done kind of client where one mistake is all it takes to sever the relationship?

Do you celebrate when things are going well? Do you offer words of affirmation or support? Are you open to sharing feedback? Are you willing to be an advocate for your VA as they are for you?

Communication is a two way street just like working together. Thinking about what you need and how you show up will help you in terms of asking questions and hearing the answers you need when someone talks with you.

Personality Styles
I'm a very relational person. I like to build long term relationships with my clients. So when I'm just getting to know a potential client, I focus on personality styles. I think it's important to know up front if we like each other. Can we listen to each other speak? Do we get along?

If the conversation is easy and goes long, that is usually a good indicator for me that we'll get along well when working together. Not everyone thinks this way and that's okay.

I can get pretty exuberant. I like to laugh and when excited tend to talk a lot and fast. I'm also a bit spiritually woo-woo (hey, I'm from California). Because of this, I worry I'm too much for super quiet people. This is not to say I don't attract and work with quiet clients. I do and they are wonderful. I just know this quality of myself so when a potential client is more introverted, I look at other qualities to determine our fit.

Consider what you need to know about your VA's personality style and how it may mesh or clash with your own.

- Are you extroverted or introverted? Do you need someone who is the same?

- Do you want to get along well or great?

- Do you want someone funny or serious?

- Do you want to become friends or stay co-workers?

- Do you need someone highly organized, a cheerleader, a go-getter or are you okay leading the way?

If your VA is client-facing, do you need them to be outgoing and friendly, professional or just competent?

Personality determines communication style and reaction to unexpected situations. Doing that introspection and knowing your business tendencies can help you find the right match.

Know your Managing Style
If you've never worked with an assistant before you may not know your managing style. I didn't. Many clients believe that a VA will step into their business and know what to do and do it. That's simply not a reasonable expectation.

Before hiring my VA, I didn't know how to work as a client or a manager. Instead of delegating the little things, I did them. The problem was that my assistant didn't learn my idiosyncrasies and if I hadn't learned how to delegate, I would always have to do the little things. Which defeats the whole purpose of having an assistant, right?

There is a learning curve to working with others. Even the most experienced VA is not a mind reader and needs time to learn your method of doing things and your eye for detail.

How you communicate this is your managing style. Are you a micromanager? Do you sweat the small stuff? Are you resistant to change? Do you often work to the last minute or have lots of time sensitive emergencies?

It's important to know how you work and what your needs are so you can communicate them efficiently with your VA.

Match Your Managing Style to Your Support

In chapter three, I talked about the different types of support. Some levels of support need more direction and processes up front by the client in order to do their best work while others can take a more intuitive approach and learn as they go. Knowing your managing style is key when deciding what kind of support you are looking for.

Do you need someone to take the wheel and help you create a process or do you have one in place already? Can you easily express your needs to your assistant or do you need a manager to translate for you?

One of my clients worked with an agency and had a team of virtual assistants. She was baffled about how to bridge the gap between herself and the team. Though one of the VAs was tasked as the team leader by the agency, she simply delegated the tasks. She didn't actually manage the communication between my client and the rest of the team. The difficulty was in my client's inability to clearly express her needs to the lead assistant in a way that could be communicated to the rest of the team. This didn't align with my client's managing style. With a team of Doers, my client needed an OBM or Collaborator VA to take the lead and manage the overall vision so the team leader could delegate the steps to the right team member.

There is a difference between being busy and productive.

A VA can check off to-do list items all day and still never get anywhere. Seeing how the tasks fit into the big picture isn't something everyone can do. It's up to the client to either express and manage the big picture or find someone who will.

It's important to note that regardless of the kind of VA you work with, your business is your business. The buck stops with you. It's up to clients to review all work, point out errors and speak up for changes. The client can not disappear and leave the handling of the business to the VA. That is not our job. We support the client to manage the tasks of their business but the business owner is the decision maker, vision holder and has the final say on everything. VAs will leave if the client becomes a ghost or doesn't take the lead.

Time Availability
The joy of being a VA is that it's a flexible job and most VAs have created their businesses in order to balance family, personal lives and work. Since a VA is not an employee, their available work hours may differ from yours. Is it important to you that they're available during your work hours or are you okay with them working on your stuff whenever they get to it?

Although my business hours are listed as Monday-Thursday 10am-4pm Pacific Time, I use the term "generally" because while I may be in the office, there are a number of things I could be working on. Just because I'm in the office doesn't mean I'm readily available. For example, I limit the amount of client work I do on Mondays so I can get a bulk of my business tasks done like writing my newsletter and invoicing. This works for my clients because as long as I get my work done, no one questions when I do it.

If you're used to working to emergencies, do you need someone at your beck-and-call? If so, a VA is probably not the right fit for you. Most VAs work with multiple clients and often cannot guarantee on-demand availability.

VAs can work anywhere in the world. How important is it to you that your VA is in your time zone or that they have work hours that match yours? Can you adjust to working within their time zone or working times?

There are pros and cons to working with VAs not in your time zone. I work in Pacific Time while most of my clients work in Eastern Time. The pro to this is I have three extra work hours at the end of their day but all our meetings tend to be later in their morning or afternoon due to my start time. My brain doesn't function until at least 8 am. My VA in the Philippines starts his day at the end of mine so he tends to have a full day of work after our calls and I usually come into the office to a slew of completed work or questions.

Security Needs

Many times a VA is privy to important and sensitive or confidential information. If that is part of your business, you need to think about your specific needs around security. Some VAs work off their dining room table with their computers in full view of family and kids. Is it going to cause issues if a family member sees them working on your stuff?

Up until September 2023, I shared my office with various family members. I didn't have the luxury of locking the door or keeping things secure. I made sure any potential client was aware of my setup before we started working together. I couldn't work with clients who needed high security. Now that I have systems in place and a door that locks, I can offer better security. However, I still avoid clients with very strict security needs that go beyond my comfort level.

Depending on your type of business, do you need a non-disclosure agreement as part of your contract with the VA to work on your projects? Does your VA need to adhere to certain ethics or codes of conduct to interact with your clients?

Things that fall under Security needs could include but aren't limited to:

- What is your comfort level with sharing passwords and log-ins? What do you need to feel comfortable sharing this information with your VA?

- Client records or contact information.

- Confidentiality- stated (like HIPAA) or perceived (what happens in Vegas, stays in Vegas).

- Bank information or credit card numbers.

- Birthdays and important dates.

- Documents, templates and branding information.

Over the years, I have had clients request addendums to my contract around confidentiality and adherence to association ethics. I will always review the requested changes and amend what is comfortable for me. As a graduate of AssistU, the virtual training program I completed when I started my business, I uphold The Pledge of Ethics[1]. I include wording with a link in my contract to provide transparency. Sometimes that is enough for clients to feel secure in my professionalism. What

---

1 AssistU Ethics Pledge: https://www.workwithava.com/ethics-pledge/

do you need to feel secure? What are your current security concerns? How might you address them? What might come up going forward?

Training

Remember that a VA could learn something new every day and still not know everything. What is your stance on paying for time spent on training?

I offer two suggestions:

- If you are asking your VA to learn a program that can only be used for your business, you should pay for training.

- If a VA can take the training of a program and apply it to other current or future clients, ask if they would be willing to share the cost of training.

I did both for a client. He was interested in using a CRM that I had heard of but didn't use. Since it was a common platform and often requested in job descriptions, I offered to split the time spent on doing a class. This worked for me because I could add that program to my skill set for future clients.

Later when he asked me to look into a different program I would only use for his business, I requested he pay for the time for me to learn to set it up. Both times he agreed.

Do you have specific programs that you want/need someone to use? If yes, are you comfortable paying for time spent on training?

Are you open to learning a new program that works the same if your VA offers it?

Today many programs work the same or act similarly. A VA may have experience in a program like the one you use but it may take them some time to learn the differences.

Customer Relationship Management tools (CRMs) often come to mind. There are so many options out there that it's highly unlikely that the one you use is the same as the one your VA knows. In the course of working with a client, I learned just enough of Honeybook to help the client with her project. Later, a different client asked me to learn Dubsado. Turns out both programs were very similar. They worked closely enough that I was able to pick up the new program with relative ease.

The same could be said about Email Marketing programs like Mailchimp, Constant Contact, MailerLite, FloDesk, or Social media scheduling tools like Hootsuite, Tweetdeck, Facebook Metasuite, and the like.

When I first started my business, email marketing was barely a thing. The only programs at that time required HTML coding except for Constant Contact which offered a user-friendly platform. I liked it so much that I became a Business Partner and trainer. Years later my clientele shifted and Mailchimp became the primary platform. Because of my skills with Constant Contact, I was able to adjust to Mailchimp with relative ease. A VA can be proficient and highly skilled in one program but those skills often translate to something similar.

Is it important to you that your VA is an expert in the programs you work with or is it enough that they have a general idea of how to get your work done and learn your programs as they go? Sometimes you may have a need that your VA doesn't know or want to learn. Is this a deal breaker or are you open to finding someone to fill in the gaps?

I often tell clients if I don't know something, I can find someone who does. Either I will connect the client and the support person to work together separately from me or I will offer to manage the project. It depends on the situation and the client.

Ask your VA what their comfort level is. Some work well with others and some want to stay hands off. Know your comfort level and have ways of communicating your needs if they don't match.

Deal Breakers
This chapter is not about identifying what will mesh and clash with you and your business as much as it is about your personality. As you go through each of these suggested considerations, look at both the positive and negative versions of qualities. Write down what you are looking for and also note any deal breakers - qualities that are absolute NOs for you.

For example, I bristle at highly militant people and Type A New York Style Go Getters. I will not work with workaholics who expect to reach what I perceive to be unattainable goals. I don't do cold calling or financials.

We are not meant to get along with everyone and that's okay. Knowing what your deal breakers are will limit the time you spend on the wrong person so you can spend your time on finding the right fit.

Sensitive topics
Working with a VA can oftentimes bring up sensitive topics.

Some of these you may not be aware will affect you until you experience them. I'm sharing some of the big ones that could come up so you can think about them and determine if they are a deal breaker for you and create a question around them.

Boundaries/ Standards

Though buzz words, we all have our own standards and boundaries. *Boundaries* are rules that determine what other people cannot do to YOU. Boundaries will be deal breakers. Rude behavior, constant or non-existent communication, and doing/not doing types of tasks may be considered boundaries. One boundary I hold is not taking client calls when I'm not working. A client can text, email or even call at any time but I won't respond until I'm back on the clock.

Standards are rules that YOU hold yourself to. Standards are how you behave towards others. I follow the Golden Rule. I underpromise and overdeliver whenever possible. I try to be honest and transparent with deadlines and mistakes. I also honor my needs and protect my downtime.

What are your standards and boundaries? How can you communicate them with your VA?

Cultural Differences

Our world is a beautiful blending of people and cultures and the beauty of working in a virtual realm is that a VA or client can be literally anywhere in the world. This brings a larger worldview and different perspectives. Some people love learning about new cultures and traditions while others prefer to stick with what they know. Neither is wrong but it is something to consider.

If working with someone from a culture different than yours, it's important to know how it may or may not align with what is normal in your culture. In her book, Beyond Wins, Mala Subramaniam explains that in some overseas cultures like India and the Philippines, a support person will not say no to a request from a person with a perceived higher status (like a boss or client). If they are given a task they are unclear on or can't do, the person will still say yes even if they are confused by the request. They may not ask for clarification which could lead to misunderstandings.

In my experience, they also tend to disappear. When I needed to learn a new-to-me program, I reached out to a VA Facebook group I was a member of to get some help. A VA responded and we had a great conversation about my needs. I paid for her time to record the tutorial videos. Then nothing. I reached out several times but the VA didn't respond and never sent the requested information. She ghosted me and I ended up needing to go through the PayPal refund department.

In some cultures where English is not the first language, they think more literally while in native English speaking cultures like the US, we may use slang or words with less literal meanings. A client asked for images "bathed in energy" and received images of shower stalls. This is not always the case but I've heard other similar stories.

Generation Gaps

Generation gaps between clients and VAs are not uncommon. I'm sandwiched between two generations- Boomers and Millennials/Gen Z. In some things, I know more than my dad but not as much as my kids. My VAs are all younger than me. This has some pros and cons.

Consider your comfort level with generational gaps. Technology and communication styles differ greatly. Consider your needs. If email is your preferred mode of communication but your VA only texts, you may have some trouble communicating.

The older generations prefer to talk on the phone, write out text messages in full grammatically correct sentences and may send an individual email for every single question they have. The younger generations use emojis to convey feelings, try to do tasks in the quickest way possible and may not always have the best attention to details. Middle generations are tech-savvy enough to try new things but may grumble while they're doing it.

Work ethics and ideology
We've all heard jokes shared around the dinner table about the differences between the generational work ethics and ideology. It's a staple in my family when my dad comes for Sunday dinner. I've seen examples where it's true and false. Every person is different regardless of their generation. What is your work ethic and ideology? Does your VA need to have the same one, complement yours, or fill in the gaps?

When I first started working with my VA, our styles were very different. I am highly detail-oriented, plan ahead and am very organized. My VA didn't catch my mistakes when copying/pasting my content into graphics and often waited until the last minute to meet a deadline. However, they were also highly organized and helped me create better systems. It took some work but we found our groove even though we're different.

Artificial Intelligence (AI) and Technology
We all have different comfort levels when it comes to the use of AI. My colleague, LeAnn, is always listening to podcasts sharing

the cutting edge uses of AI and puts tips into her newsletter while I can barely use ChatGPT to help with starting a blog post.

Technology in all its uses is dependent on each user's comfort and preference. Since working with a VA depends on web-based technology, it's important to consider your comfort level and what relationship you want to have with AI and other programs and software.

Gender/Sexual Orientation

Having grown up in California and spending a large chunk of time in the theater community, I'm pretty open minded about the LGBTQIA+ community. One of my VAs is non-binary and another is a gay man. Both are amazing people and do fantastic work for me. I'm not telling anyone reading this book what to think or how to act but be honest with yourself. If you feel a certain way about gender issues or sexual orientations, consider a respectful way to communicate a yes or no.

Politics and Religion

In recent years, politics and religion have become divisive topics in many spheres. Unless it's brought up to me, I don't talk to anyone about either. It is not because I don't have my own thoughts and feelings but because, in my opinion, neither topic belongs in a professional setting. For me, it doesn't matter who you voted for in the last election or how you worship. For others, these values can be deal breakers. Be honest with yourself. If it matters to you, create a quality for it.

Hobbies

Consider what you like to do outside of your business. Are you an avid hiker? Closet romance reader? Football aficionado?

All virtual assistants will respect the businesses they work with professionally but if you want an added layer of interest that aligns with your business, consider that. VAs tend to niche into areas they're passionate about so finding a VA who is passionate about your business is a plus.

I have connected to my clients on deeper levels because of my outside interests. For instance, one of my clients is a writer. We can relate on that level because I'm a writer too. Another client and I connected on our shared work history in theater. I love working with coaches because I am passionate about the ripple effect. The skills I bring to my clients allow them to bring their skills to their clients and so the impact of working together flows out into the wider world.

Experience vs. Years in Business
Years in business don't always equate to years of experience. I have a couple of VA colleagues who spent many years as stay-at-home moms. One homeschooled her kids. On paper, they may not have the "experience" of working in typical administrative businesses but as any mother will tell you, they have plenty of skills. Maintaining and running a home and family is way more intense than some of the most demanding corporate CEOs. Many of life's experiences translate to a person being able to handle crisis, become master problem-solvers, hold great compassion for others, and be highly organized.

Interviewing a VA is not like interviewing an employee where you look at their resume and search for keywords. Many VAs don't supply a resume.

Depending on the type of VA you are looking for, you may want to ask how many years in business they have or how their life experience has shaped how they work with clients. There are many Doers who are just starting out in both work and life who are hungry to learn. Consider if you need the experience, want the time in business, or are open to learning with your VA.

Take Action

Now is the time to look at your business and make a list of the qualities you're looking for in a successful candidate. I recommend writing down the qualities in positive terms and shifting any negatives to a positive or neutral tone.

Here is a list of ten examples:
- Organized
- Detail Oriented
- Proactive
- Reliable
- Professional
- Empathetic
- Resourceful
- Adaptable
- Self-Motivated
- Has a Positive Attitude

I put a list of **100+ Qualities to Look for in a VA** in the Resources webpage.

Once you start meeting with VAs, it may come down to a feeling rather than who looks best on paper. Having an idea of what you're looking for will help you tune into those vibrations and dig a little deeper. Looking honestly at the qualities you want in your VA can be exhausting work. Pat yourself on the back for doing it. You are one step closer to finding your perfect fit!

Recap: Key Points

- **Finding the Right Fit:**
Selecting a VA is like dating. You need to look beyond the profile to get to know the person. Interview multiple candidates to ensure compatibility beyond the task list.

- **Prioritizing Communication Styles:**
Effective communication requires understanding preferences like email, phone, or text and addressing potential challenges (e.g., tone or response time). Flexibility and open dialogue are key to resolving issues and building trust.

- **Matching Personality Styles:**
Consider whether you want a VA who shares your personality traits or complements them. Compatibility in areas like organization, extroversion/introversion, or leadership styles can impact the working relationship.

- **Time Availability and Expectations:**
A VA's schedule might differ from yours. Decide if it's essential for them to work during your hours or if asynchronous work is acceptable. Clarify time zone preferences and turnaround times upfront.

- **Security and Confidentiality:**
Evaluate your needs regarding data security, confidentiality, and physical workspace setup. Consider NDAs, ethical adherence, and comfort levels with sharing sensitive information or passwords.

- **Adaptability and Training:**
Acknowledge that VAs often learn new skills regularly. Decide if you're willing to pay for training on specific programs or adapt to the tools they already use.

- **Identifying Gaps and Needs:**
Reflect on your weaknesses and business challenges to find a VA whose strengths fill those gaps. For example, if you lack organization, look for a detail-oriented assistant.

- **Passion and Alignment:**
Consider whether you want a VA who is not just professional but also passionate about your industry or business goals. Many VAs specialize in niches that align with their interests.

- **Crafting a Qualities List:**
Write down the traits and qualities you desire in a VA in positive terms. Use this list as a guide during interviews and trust your instincts when making the final decision.

Journal Prompts

What qualities or characteristics, beyond cost, do I value most in someone I work with?

What gaps in my business or skills could a VA help fill and what qualities would make someone a perfect fit for these areas?

How can I identify whether a VA aligns with these traits during an interview?

Chapter Six

Finding the Right Fit

Up to this point, we've been focusing on foundational pieces like handoff lists, budgets, types of virtual assistants, and important qualities. Now it's time to put all the pieces together to ask the right questions to find the perfect fit for you and your business. Once you do this, you can start looking for candidates.

Where do I find VAs?

Like you would for any job, craft an ideal candidate job description. Take all your elements and write out what you're looking for and any specific needs you have. Make sure you can clearly express what you're looking for.

Unlike in 2005 when I was starting, there are virtual assistants everywhere and people now know someone or know someone who knows someone.

Share your job description with friends and family and ask if they know anyone. Post your request on social media, mention your need in networking groups, or try my **Find a VA** program.

Make sure the referrals you collect are good quality. One of my clients received my name from another client. She said he was very specific about why he was referring her to me and, even more importantly, why I would be the right VA for her. Sometimes the reasons someone gives for that person being awesome is not awesome to you. If possible, ask the person giving you a referral for specifics about their recommendation.

For some new business owners, they may not have the network or community of business colleagues to draw on for referrals. This is one of the reasons I started my Find a VA program. Whenever a new business owner crossed my path, it was second nature for me to hear their needs and offer referrals. Straddling both worlds as a client and VA puts me in a unique position to connect my network of pre-qualified virtual assistants with potential clients. VAs are looking for clients just as clients are looking for VAs.

I built my VA Referral Directory because it is my core belief that there is a right fit for everyone. If I'm not the one, I may know someone who is. I also encourage VAs to connect with other VAs to expand their networks for skills, support and referrals.

Please note that many wonderful and highly qualified VAs will promote their work on sites like UpWork, Fiverr and the like. These VAs tend to be more project focused than relationship building. These are not the VAs I am referring to in this book. My focus is on relationship driven VAs who are looking to collaborate long term with clients.

Many live in countries where the US dollar goes a lot further and can charge less. If you're looking for someone to do a quick and easy project or if this is where your budget takes you, make sure to read their reviews, look through their work portfolios, and talk with them before hiring.

A word of caution. These sites are also rife with scammers or providers who show up well in the interview process and then disappear. It's important that you don't take any conversations or pay for any work off the platform. For example, if you're communicating with a VA on Fiverr, keep the conversation and transactions on Fiverr. These sites have strict guidelines as to how they can protect users and you may not be protected if you take things off the platform. Remember that you get what you pay for. Cheap help is not always inexpensive.

VA Training Organizations

If you're not having luck with your network, check out VA training organizations. These organizations usually have some kind of directory or program for graduate members to participate in for job leads. In most cases, this directory is free for potential clients.

A list of VA Training organizations and their directories is on the Resources webpage. Each site has a questionnaire to answer. Some are longer and more in-depth than others. Regardless of the site you apply to, check out the questions ahead of time and deliberate on your responses before adding them to submit your Request for Proposal. This will be your first impression to any VA receiving your submission. Put your best foot forward. Consider how you would like someone to answer the questions if they were applying for a job in your company.

When I first graduated from my training program, I joined The Registry which is AssistU's version of a directory. The client side questionnaire was very in depth and judging by the responses, I could determine if we would be a good fit before I sent a proposal letter.

For many VAs this request determines whether they will respond to your submission. They are reading your answers with an eye toward fit. If they don't like what you write, they will not respond to your request.

Once you start getting responses from your Requests for Proposals, read through them and decide who you want to talk with. This is your first impression of the VA. Jot down any pros or cons so you can ask about them later.

- What is your initial vibe from the tone of their response?

- Do any of your ideal qualities jump out?

- Do they seem excited to work with you?

- What have they highlighted that stands out to you?

- Is there a sense of ease or security in taking the next steps?

Do some additional research. Take a look at their website and/or social media to learn more about them. What attracts you? What deters you?

Interviewing Process
Unlike hiring an employee, a virtual assistant is business to business. Each client and interview situation is unique. Have a list of questions to ask and what responses will feel right. Trust

your instincts. Remember to interview more than one VA and go with the best fit for your business. Like you, they are looking for the perfect partner for their business. As much as you are interviewing them, they are interviewing you.

Regardless of whether you're the one leading or sitting on the other side of the table, the interview process can be scary for anyone. As the client, you're invested in finding someone to join you in building your business. As the VA, they're invested in making sure they don't screw up your business. Either way, you're both looking for the right partner to spend hours a month working with.

Go into the experience with both levity and a sense of humor. Some VAs will have a process they take potential clients through and some won't. I know I learned my process in my training program and often guided potential clients from introduction to signing the contract. However, when I met my first VA, they did not have a process to take me through. They left it up to me to lead the way.

Not all VAs take on clients the same way. You must have an idea of what your process may look like and what questions you need to ask so you get answers for all YOUR important needs. My process has evolved over the years. I've had client discovery calls that went so long they morphed right into the initial interview topics. By the end, we knew we were a fit but I still encouraged those clients to talk to other VAs and come back if the magic was still there. I am sharing my process as an example. Take what works for you and leave the rest.

This section is a guide for you to create a process in the event that the VAs you meet do not have an interview process.

Take Action

In my training program, I was taught to take clients through a three-part interview process. Here is an outline I recommend. You are free to adjust it however works for you. Write your process down including any questions that make sense to ask in each step.

1. **Discovery Call-** 15-30 minute get-to-know-you call is like meeting for coffee.

2. **Initial Interview Call-** 60-minute call to discuss the basics.

3. **Deeper Interview Call-** 60-90 minute deeper call to discuss more value driven topics.

Consider the following:
No matter how a potential client comes to me, before they get time on my calendar I ask them some pre-qualifying questions to judge our initial fit.

These questions are:

- Briefly describe your business. What do you do?

- What are you struggling with that led you to decide to start the search to work with a virtual assistant?

- Have you ever worked with a VA before? If so, how was the experience (what worked well and what didn't)?

- Do you have a clear idea of the tasks you would have for a VA should you hire one? If so, what are they? If you're not sure, don't worry.

- Why is now the right time to work with a virtual assistant?

- When are you looking to start working with a VA?

- How did you hear about me?

How a business owner answers these questions tells me a lot about them. Based on their responses, I can decide if we should schedule a Discovery call. Either way, I respond with next steps and my scheduling link or a quick "I'm not the right fit" email.

When someone responds to your post or is referred to you, what do you need to know in order to set up a Discovery Call?

Check out websites and social media like you would a dating profile. Are there enough pros for you to swipe right or too many cons? Are there any questions that would indicate a deal breaker right up front? If not, schedule a Discovery call.

Discovery Call

Like meeting for coffee or drinks gives you a quick and safe way to engage without the pressure of a long date, use a Discovery Call to see if you like talking to each other. You can keep it shallow and avoid talking about work or you could ask any deal breaker questions or ask about your non-negotiable task items. If you don't enjoy the conversation, their responses or the VA doesn't do what you need, you save yourself time getting too attached. What are your non-negotiables?

Some Discovery Call questions:
- Tell me about your business. How did you get into it? What do you like about it?

- Do you have any hobbies?

- Are you comfortable talking about yourself and getting to know co-workers on a personal level?

- Is the work I need the work you do?

If the call goes well, move on to the initial interview.

Initial Interview

Here is when you get down to business. Now you're on your first date. Use this call to talk about practical issues and the logistics of working together. Discuss your business such as the current state, tasks you like doing and those you want to delegate, your current processes and what you would do if you had the time and space from not doing them, long/short term goals, communication style, what working with a VA means to you and share some info about yourself personally and your work style. Ask the VA questions about themselves, their business and how they work including office hours, fees, skills they can/can't do, and any of their standards/ boundaries. What do you want to make sure to share or learn during this call? What qualities would you like your VA to have? What questions do you need to ask to discover those qualities?

Some initial interview questions that you can ask:
- What inspired you to become a VA and what do you love most about being a VA?

- Who are the types of clients you enjoy working with most?

- How does your business typically operate? These are things like your hours, fees, or holiday schedule.

- Given my hand-off list, how do you imagine we could work together and what kinds of tasks could you take off my plate?

- Based on what you've seen with other clients, how many hours do you think would make the biggest difference in my workload?

If the logistics are covered and you want to continue, schedule a second call for more deeper discussion questions. For some VAs, they will start working with clients at this point and do not do a deeper discussion interview call. If the fit is not right at this point, continue your search.

Deeper Discussion
This is an optional call but 90 minutes should cover it. This is dinner and a movie. You may already know this person is the one. These questions can also be sprinkled along as you work together to grow and build trust. During this call discuss any deeper topics that are important to you like your values and ethics.

Some deeper discussion questions could be:
- How do you typically manage large or complex projects? Do you plan everything out in advance or do you thrive under tight deadlines?

- Do you prefer close collaboration with clients or do you work better independently once clear goals are set?

- How do you prefer to receive feedback or constructive criticism from clients?

- If you were feeling overwhelmed or needed extra support, how would you bring that up?

By the end of this call, you'll know if you are working together or moving on. If you both agree to work together, start your onboarding process which we'll discuss in the next chapter.

Additional **Interview Questions** are found on the Resources webpage. More importantly, look at your qualities list and draft questions around your needs.

When I considered what I was looking for in my ideal client, I used my Interview questions from the Virtual Training Program, as well as points assembled by Anastacia Brice[1], and created this quality list:

- My clients can afford to work with me long term.

- My clients honor my work hours and do not expect me to be available at their beck and call.

- My clients value me, the work I do and any feedback I offer.

- My clients value my time and show up for me.

- Mistakes happen and my clients are open to learning from them rather than placing blame.

- My clients have minimal security needs because my family has access to my work space.

1- Based on *"Dance Lessons: Six Steps to Great Partnership in Business and Life"* by Chip Bell and Heather Shea.

I crafted an assessment that asked questions in a way that I could determine if we were a good fit.

On a scale of *1= "Never true of me"* through *5= "Absolutely true of me"*, I asked questions like:

- I pay my bills on time.

- I can absolutely afford to pay for VA services long term.

- I expect my VA to be available whenever I need her.

- I welcome suggestions that could improve my business.

- On time for me is within 5 minutes before or after a scheduled appointment time.

- I understand that mistakes happen but I'd rather learn from them than place blame.

- I subscribe to the notion that children should be seen and not heard.

And more.

Having a list of questions to ask is a great start but you also need to listen for the right answers. Ask open ended questions that get the person talking.

While a VA may not self identify with my definitions of Doer VA or Collaborator VA, you can deduce what type of VA someone is by the way they answer questions.

Doer VAs tend to respond with "tell me what to do" or "I can do that." Collaborator VAs are more solution oriented and will likely offer suggestions or say things like, "here's how I can help with that" or "what we can do is."

While the interview process will help you narrow down the right fit, sometimes the best way to find a VA is to trust your gut or intuition. Someone who looks great on paper may not feel right while someone who doesn't necessarily do all the tasks you're looking for may be exactly right in all other ways.

One of my clients was not a match for me on paper. However, there was something about the way he answered my questionnaire and responded to my email that made me schedule the Discovery Call. The feeling of rightness was almost immediate for both of us. We even agreed to "try it out and see where things took us." Even though on paper we didn't match, two years later we're still working together.

Go with the person who makes the most sense for your business. It's my opinion that fit trumps anything else. Like in dating, you can't fake chemistry. The right VA will feel right even if they don't do everything you think you need them to. Remember that the right VA can get the work done even if they are not the one to do it.

You're getting so close to working with a VA. This is such an individual process. You're taking the time to discover the ins and outs of finding the right fit for your business. Give yourself a high-five for all the work you've done so far. It's a lot and you're doing it!!

In the next chapter we'll discuss what you need once you find your VA.

Recap: Key Points

- **Finding VAs:**
  Leverage personal networks such as friends, family, and social media for referrals.

  Consider VA-specific resources like directories or training organization programs that match clients with VAs based on their needs.

- **First Impressions Matter:**
  Treat your Request for Proposal as a job application. It's often a VA's first impression of you. Thoughtful and detailed responses can attract the right candidates.

  Be prepared for potential VAs to have their own questionnaires or processes for pre-qualifying clients.

- **Mutual Fit:**
  The VA-client relationship is business-to-business. Both parties are assessing compatibility.

  Approach interviews as a mutual evaluation process focusing on finding the right match rather than simply hiring based on tasks or rates.

- **Step-by-Step Interview Process:**
Start with a brief initial conversation to establish basic compatibility and interest. Go deeper from there.

Tailor your questions to uncover the the qualities you value most in a VA. It may take a couple of calls.

- **Flexibility and Fit Over Tasks:**
A strong professional and personal fit may outweigh task-specific capabilities. Skills can often be learned or delegated.

Prioritize the candidate who aligns with your business needs, values, and working style over someone who simply fits your task list.

- **Iterative Decision-Making:**
Interview more than one candidate to compare options.

Use each step of the process to decide whether to continue or move on and refine your understanding of what works for you.

Trust your gut. Sometimes the best fit may not check all task-related boxes but feels right overall.

Journal Prompts

What are my non-negotiables when it comes to hiring a VA and why are these particular aspects important for my business?

Do I know anyone in my network that can help me find a VA?

What interview process do I want to create?

Chapter Seven

You Found a VA! *Now What?*

Let's pretend you've found your virtual assistant! Woohoo!
Congratulations!

Now what?

Getting started can be fun and a little overwhelming in the beginning. Most of the time a VA will let the client lead the onboarding process.

Onboarding means getting your assistant up to speed as quickly as possible with all the details they need to start working on your stuff. If your VA has their own onboarding process, they will typically communicate this with you after the interview process when you've agreed to work together.

As we've talked about in other chapters, not all VAs are the same. Some have learned from years of experience and offer solutions to potential problems because they've lived through the mistakes and others have never felt the sting of those mistakes and will learn along with you.

When it comes to the process of onboarding your VA, you may not know what you need, have any processes in place, or choose to work with a VA who doesn't either. The beautiful thing is that you can learn as you go. Ask questions. Encourage your VA to ask questions. Create an environment where you both feel safe to build the foundation as you go. If you've never worked with an assistant before, this can feel awkward and uncomfortable.

Put on your business owner hat and step into your leadership role. This may require you to gain a different clarity of how you want your business to run but, over time, you'll grow the confidence required to delegate your tasks. You may need to step out of your comfort zone to look at all aspects of your business with an eye towards realism. Just go at the pace you and your VA are comfortable with and talk through any snags that show up along the way. You will learn while your VA learns and together you'll figure out what works for your business and working relationship.

Start with what you're comfortable handing off and what will be needed to make that happen. The client brings the WHAT so the VA can be the resource for the HOW.

A VA can't take over a task you don't hand off. If it's all in your head how you do a certain thing AND you want it done that way all the time, you will need to figure out how to communicate it in a way your VA will understand. Once the thoughts are out of your head, your VA can document the process for you.

A few years ago, I worked with a handful of entrepreneurs going through a virtual summit program. I had never done a summit before and neither had any of them. We were all learning together. By the end of the last summit, I could do all the preparations for the event in my sleep and crafted a checklist and process for the inevitability that someone would want to do a summit again.

When another client asked me to help with a workshop (not a summit) I was able to reuse my checklist and guide them through this new territory. When a friend asked me about the back end of hosting a summit, I could tell her how long it would take, how many VA hours to budget for and point out the hidden energy and time requirements. She was very grateful because she hadn't considered much beyond the event itself.

Onboarding Process Considerations
Start by asking the following questions:

- What is important for you to have in place *BEFORE* you start working with someone?

- Do you have established processes with your clients? If yes, what elements can be adjusted for your assistant to take over?

- Do you have a contract? Do you need one?

- Do you need a non-disclosure agreement?

- What project(s) do you want to start with?

- What information, access or training will your VA need to complete it?

- For your program accounts, can a VA be added as a collaborator, admin, team member, or moderator with their own login OR will they need to log in as you to accomplish your tasks?

- Do you have the login information easily accessible?

- What information do you need to collect from your VA for accounting and tax purposes?

- How do you plan to share any necessary files?

- How will you share sensitive information like passwords?

All of these questions and more are part of your onboarding process.

Contracts

Do you have a contract for working with contractors? Do you need one? I'm not a lawyer and cannot offer legal advice. However, I feel it's important to have your own simple contract especially if your chosen VA doesn't have one. It's up to you and your comfort level if you wish to have a contract filled with legalese set up by an attorney or a simple working agreement.

The contract should define the terms of your relationship including:

- The agreed services to be provided

- The expected working hours or deliverables

- The agreed-upon rate and payment schedule

- What payment method will be used? (PayPal, Zelle, check, etc.)

- How will sick days and vacation days be handled?
- How much notice for vacation days is needed?
- Which holidays will be observed?

Does your VA need to be from your country?

(Some US based companies require US based VAs.) If your VA is from a different country or culture than you, will they observe your holidays as well as their own? If yes, what are they and how will those dates be communicated?

How will disagreements be handled?

Is there a probationary period? How long?

What happens if one of you wants out of the relationship? Do you require advance notice? How much?

What process will be required to end the relationship?

Do you have specifics to add like a confidentiality clause?

Adding a Non-Disclosure Clause or agreement to your contract helps to protect your business assets like passwords, client lists, and business processes. Include wording forbidding your VA to share your sensitive information with other parties unless given express consent by you.

My contract is actually a Policies and Procedures document. It outlines all the above in pretty friendly wording. Some of my clients signed my agreement as is but a couple have asked for addendums or edits. Any changes to the agreement are part of the onboarding process but once the contract is signed, all parties should operate within the parameters.

When I hired my first VA, they didn't have a contract so I adjusted my agreement for the flipside to protect myself.

Afterwards, my VA created their own and I was happy to sign it.

Company-specific Branding:
Now that you're growing your team, ask yourself:

- Will my VA communicate directly with my clients? How do I want that to look?

- Should my VA use their personal email address or will I provide a business branded email? With company branded emails available, your VA can professionally communicate on your behalf. These emails usually look like [name]@companyURL.com or Info@, Admin@, hello@, or any version that fits your company culture. Not all companies use these types of branded emails and opt for free emails like Gmail, Yahoo, Hotmail, etc.

- Do I know how to set one up or do I need someone else to do it?

- Is there a specific branding or signature they should use?

Know and Document your Processes
When it comes to running a business, working with a VA, or just getting stuff done, there is a process to productivity. It's important to know your processes and procedures before trying to hand them off to someone else.

What does Process and Procedures mean?

Though these terms are closely related and often used together or interchangeably, there is a real difference between them.

Process – "The What" – a series of actions or steps taken to achieve a particular end. Knowing what you've got on your plate and having a process of staying current on all your open project loops and to-dos lets you know where you need help. Documenting the steps to complete the regularly recurring tasks gives you a playbook if you're in the market to hire a VA or thinking of adding a team member.

Procedure– "The How" – a specific documented set of steps or actions to carry out the process in order to complete a task or achieve a specific goal. Procedures are often used to ensure consistency and efficiency in operations.

Think of the process as a workflow chart giving you the steps you need to complete to achieve your end result while the procedure consists of the individual steps. For example, this is my process for social media:

When considering handing off any task, it's important that YOU know what the steps are and that you can share them effectively and communicate why they may be important to you. When I handed off social media to my VA, we adjusted my process to include additional steps. I like a lot of communication. When my VA creates the graphics for my social media, he alerts me in our Google Doc that the images are ready for review so I can share my approval or edits. With my approval, he can schedule the posts. If I was doing this task by myself, those steps would be deleted.

Before you spend lots of time creating an intricately detailed process, consider your VA's learning style preference. Ask if they prefer quick verbal directions, video tutorials or written manuals. Their response may surprise you and save you lots of time and energy.

One of my clients felt so relieved when I turned her from *"OMG I have to develop this training module for Rachael"* to *"record yourself doing stuff on Loom."* Make this easy on yourself. Your VA will ask for more help if they need it.

Here are some tips to start documenting your process to create your procedures:

- **Record a video:** This does not need to be perfect or shown to anyone but your VA. Using any video recording software like Loom, Zoom, WeVideo, iMovie, or whatever you prefer, share your screen, click record and go through your process as you normally would. As you go through your steps, verbalize what you're doing and why each step is important. Note anything that could be helpful information for your VA to know about your thought process and needs.

- **Create a workflow chart:** Map out your workflow, draw it on paper or use a tool like PowerPoint or Canva to create a visual representation of your process (like my example above).

- **After you've mapped out your process, get specific on each step.** Use your recording to highlight those steps that might feel awkward but are necessary for you like sending emails to notify you that the step is complete. Also include links to any documents or programs you use.

If we use my graphic as an example, the procedure could look like this:

Step one: Create Content
Open Google Doc (link to existing doc).
Copy/paste content to use or write new content.
Add links to resources, blog post
Send an email to client for edits/approval.

Step two: Create Graphic
Open Canva - link to existing file or create a new one.
Duplicate image/create new one.
Pick an image.
Add text.
Add logo.
Save as .png file to download folder, or to a specific folder with an included link.

Step three: Write Caption
Using the content document (link here), create caption.
Add graphic image.
Add hashtags.
Add links.
Add status - ie. scheduled, posted, drafted, waiting on client approval.

Step four: Schedule post to social media platform
Open program [FB Meta Business Suite, Buffer, Hootsuite, Smarterqueue].
Draft post and copy content into it.
Schedule once approved.

Step five: Add scheduled post to spreadsheet
    Open spreadsheet [include link]
    Paste caption and upload/copy/paste image

Like I said, if you're doing the work yourself you'll likely be able to skip some of these steps but if you're handing this off to a VA, make sure to add any steps specific for communication or ask that your VA help you fill in any gaps.

One of my clients came to me with amazing processes and documentation. It was easy for me to take over because all of the steps were clearly labeled and every procedure was full of links and resources. The instructions were streamlined, concise and made the process a breeze. When he asked what I could take over, I quickly tagged the pieces I could do. He felt immediate relief when he saw how many steps I could take over.

For me, this client was an exception and not the rule. Not every client will be or needs to be that organized. Your process and procedures may be a quick email, only the video links, or on the job training so your VA can create the documentation. In fact, sometimes your VA can help you streamline your process or if you're open to it, they can do things their own way which may make more sense than the way you've been doing them.

Keep your documents in a secure place. If you're planning to share them, use an online file sharing app like Google Drive, OneDrive or Dropbox or use collaboration tools like Google Docs so your VA can easily be added.

Specific programs and how to access them
From your processes and project list, note any programs or software your VA will use on your behalf. What programs

(including social media platforms, CRM, Email Marketing, etc.) do you use that your VA will need to use? How will your VA log in? Will it be as you, a moderator, admin or can you create their own login credentials?

Sharing of passwords - How will you share passwords?
For security purposes, look into password vaults like 1Password or LastPass. They offer ways for clients to share passwords without the VA seeing what they are.

Since most programs now require a two-step verification process (codes sent to verify login), having a list of programs a VA will access and handling the login verification process during your first call will make getting started smoother.

Graphic Design
Graphics play a part in many areas of business from social media to headers on emails. Business owners spend lots of money to have logos created. Some have specific colors and fonts that make all their branded content look cohesive.

If your VA is doing graphic design work for you, do you have your branding colors, logos, and other branded elements ready? Will your VA use their design program or yours and who retains ownership of created content?

One of my clients asks me to transfer ownership of anything I create in our shared Google Drive folders. For other clients, I keep everything in a Dropbox folder that I invite them to. If our relationship ends, it's easy for me to remove myself from the folder and the client has all their stuff.

Collaboration Shared Drives (Google, Dropbox, OneDrive)
Communicating via email is great but sometimes it gets hard to find files or updated documents in the long thread of replies.

There are many options online to keep your working documents in one place and work collaboratively. Decide on how you will share files, documents, and artwork with your VA. Who will set up the folder? Does it matter who retains ownership of any files created and shared? Who pays for extra storage in the event of space issues?

It is highly recommended that the client creates the shared folder and shares it with their VA. This allows you to retain ownership of the folder and its contents and easily remove a VA at the end of a relationship. Google Drive allows you to create a common folder and you can work collaboratively using the Google versions of Word, Excel and Powerpoint. If this is too technical for you, ask your VA to help.

What else can your VA help you with?
Are there any business associates or family members your VA will be in contact with on a regular basis? If so, who are they and what is their contact information? Include the context of how and why your VA will interact with them. Make sure to introduce your VA to anyone on that list.

If you need your VA to be a reminder service, in what way and what information will your VA need to help with? For example, will you need them to remember family members' birthdays or client anniversaries?

Enter your VA's details into your contacts, accounting software and (if using online banking) set them up via Zelle or make sure you have the correct Venmo, PayPal or other payment account.

Start a Procedure document and put it in your shared folder. Set up an In Case of Emergency process for your VA and family in case one of you becomes incapacitated.

Add scheduled check in calls to your calendar.

Accounting/Financial

I'm not a professional and can not give tax advice. When hiring your first assistant, it's a good idea to reach out to your accountant or a tax professional in your area to ask what information you need to collect or track to be ready for tax time including what you might need for other countries. VAs are contractors. In the US, contractors need to receive a 1099 form at the end of the year for monies received over $600. What you need may also depend on what kind of company you have (sole proprietor, Corporation, LLC, etc), how you pay your VA and where your VA is located.

Have a way to track your payments to your new hire. You can use Quickbooks, invoicing/expense tracking software, or a spreadsheet. A quick call or email to your accountant should give you the answers you need for your unique situation.

What specific needs does your business have? What do you need to do?

Don't worry. You don't need to know all the answers up front! Just considering the above will make getting started so much easier.

Onboarding Overview:

- Onboarding is about getting your VA up to speed quickly with the tools, information, and processes they need.

- Clients typically lead the process but VAs with their own onboarding systems will communicate those after the interview phase.

Preparation for Onboarding:

- Establish what information and access your VA will need such as login credentials, training, or process documentation.

- Identify a starting project and ensure relevant resources (e.g., passwords, shared folders) are ready.

- Consider how to securely share sensitive information like using tools such as LastPass or 1Password.

Contracts and Agreements:

- It's important to have a contract that defines the working relationship including tasks, rates, payment schedules, and terms for vacation, holidays, or termination.

Business-Specific Considerations:

- Decide if your VA will communicate with clients using their own email or a branded business email and define any branding requirements.

- If applicable, provide branding assets (like logos or color palettes) for design tasks.

- Identify other team members or business contacts your VA will interact with and their roles.

Financial and Tax Responsibilities:
- Most VAs are independent contractors so you'll need to track payments for tax purposes.

- Consult with an accountant to ensure compliance with tax requirements based on your business structure (e.g., LLC, sole proprietor).

Establishing Processes:
- Create a shared procedure document for ongoing reference and update it regularly.

- Set up scheduled check-ins with your VA to ensure alignment and address any issues early.

Additional Tips:
- Start an "In Case of Emergency" protocol to handle unexpected situations.

- Trust that you don't need to have every detail figured out at the start. Onboarding is an evolving process.

Journal Prompts

What processes, tools, or information do I already have in place to help a VA get started? Are there areas where I feel unprepared or uncertain and how can I address them?

What would a successful onboarding experience look like for both me and my VA?

What expectations do I have for communication, workflow, and deliverables in the first 30 days?

What specific measures can I put in place to ensure the confidentiality and security of my business data? How comfortable am I with my current contract and NDA setup and is there anything I would like to refine or clarify?

Chapter Eight

Shifting From Solopreneur To Teampreneur

"A dream is a wish your heart makes"
— Songwriters Mack David,
Al Hoffman & Jerry Livingston

Throughout the book we have focused on what you need to do to implement working with a VA and there is more to getting started. Before we get into that, I wanted to circle back to your WHY.

Why did you start reading this book in the first place?

At the beginning of this journey, there was a version of you who had a dream and realized in order to achieve it, you needed help. You could no longer go it alone. All along the way we've focused on the tangibles but let's revisit the intangible. What is your vision for your business, your vision for your life and your vision for your future?

You may not be able to look that far ahead right now and you may not believe me when I say that hiring a VA will change your life but it's true.

When I took the leap to hire my first VA, I had far off dreams. You know, those ideas that feel too far away to ever come to fruition. Filling my business with ideal clients and doing a podcast were as big as I allowed myself to dream. Even knowing how I helped my clients achieve their goals, I couldn't envision how I would do it for myself.

My VA stepped in to help. Together we learned how to work together and I adjusted my vision for my business focusing solely on adding the podcast. With my VA's support, that dream became a reality and now (at the time of this writing) we're done recording Season 3 and have Season 4 planned out. My VA learned more than they could have imagined and transitioned from admin to podcast manager. Creative downloads of ideas that never occurred to me started popping into my head. I had so many that I had to expand my team in order to implement them all like this book, a VA Referral Directory, a membership community and a Find a VA program with options for all my clients' needs from referrals to coaching.

When I started my Find a VA journey, I could never have imagined the business I have now or the person I've become along the way.

I want this for you, dear reader.

I want you to do more, dream more and be more than you can imagine. Finding your VA is just a first step on your path to greatness.

That may sound scary but growth is scary. However, you don't have to go it alone. Ever! A VA (even if you have to kiss a few frogs to find the right fit) can help you break your big vision down to manageable tasks. You will never leap from here to Future You without going on the journey and facing the trials and struggles that force you to grow into the version of you that can live your dream.

Who do you need to become to have the life and business of your dreams?

Remembering why you started this journey in the first place will help you set your intention of how you work with your VA. It's not as simple as hiring a VA and stepping away. Before you start with your VA, make sure you have or create time to show up for your VA as often or infrequently as needed. Also communicate to them how you need them to show up for you.

Once your VA has been onboarded, it's time to get to work. Step into your role as captain, set your ship on course and guide your first mate to help you start making your dream a reality.

Make sure you're prepared. As you go along, the steps become second nature and the rough edges smooth out. Your comfort level grows, you start giving away more tasks, and your projects ease from survival to growth.

A VA will always need you to manage your business.

It takes time, effort and communication.

Schedule time to organize your thoughts.
It is true that a VA will take tasks off your plate. A VA will save

you time. However, the work they do for you is only as good as the prep work you do for them. Block time in your schedule so you can organize your thoughts and tasks. This can take 20 minutes to one hour. As you and your VA get more comfortable, your VA may start creating your call agendas for you.

For some clients, I meet with them 2x a week, weekly and monthly. Between calls, I track anything that comes up into a shared document so we have an agenda to talk about. They can add anything that comes up on their end and I make sure I get all my questions answered.

For my VA team calls, I look at the tasks from the client perspective. What do I need them to do? Is this a new type of task that will require explanation or is this just a check in?

Taking the time to clarify the task in your mind makes explaining and directing your VA so much easier. In the beginning, check in often to manage expectations. It's better to overcommunicate than make mistakes from lack of communication.

Start small and build trust.
Remember what we talked about in Chapter Two when creating your hand-off list. Start with small projects that tell you if the fit is right and build trust or start with the tasks that are bothering you the most.

Starting small allows you to feel each other out and gauge realistically how well you communicate, how quickly your tasks get done, and if the relationship is working out.

Grow with your VA. It's okay to grow as you learn. At first, you know what you know. Learn what you need to know for the situation at hand. Reflect on the lessons learned (good and bad). Look at them with curiosity rather than judgment and adjust going forward.

The Universe likes to fill a void.
I've seen it happen with hundreds of clients. Clearing space leads to creative downloads that guide you along the journey of your business. Clients have created programs, written books, shifted direction into their Zone of Genius, and established more work to life balance. They did it all with the help of a VA.

What are you ready to create?

You don't need to start there. If you're feeling overwhelmed or not creative, start with handing off one thing. As your comfort grows, hand off another thing and so on.

Clearing pebbles is removing the small obstacles that keep you from going after bigger dreams. As you hand off the small things, you grow more confident. As your confidence grows, you feel ready to tackle bigger things.

This is how the rest of your journey unfolds. When you're in a state of overwhelm, you can't dream bigger. That's okay. Someday you'll have created the time and space for those bigger dreams to reveal themselves. You'll be better prepared to answer the call.

Take time to reflect on the progress you're making with your VA. Once you've handed off one task or project to your VA, check in with yourself. How did it feel? How easy or difficult is it for you? How supported do you feel?

Be honest with yourself. If things aren't working as smoothly as you'd like, are you the bottleneck in the relationship? Are you hoarding tasks that would be better handed off? Are you communicating clearly? Are you showing up prepared so your VA can do their best work? If not, adjust.

Managing Expectations

I once heard that anyone can be on their best behavior for about 6-8 weeks before their true personality starts to show. By the 8th week, the new relationship excitement bubble bursts. That's partly the reason why I recommend giving yourself a three month trial period with your VA.

In the beginning, it's common for clients and VAs to step over their boundaries in order to close the sale. This is especially true with newbie VAs anxious to get a client and clients in a state of urgency to have help. Either side or both may ignore warning signs in order to relieve the pain. Over time, this causes issues. This doesn't always mean the relationship is over. It just may require you to take a closer look.

I speak from experience. When I was first starting out, I needed income. The transition plan my husband and I so clearly thought through fell apart. My husband's job (the one that would float us while I built my business) disappeared. So I filled my practice right away with less than ideal clients. I didn't even take potential clients through an interview process. Could I do the work? Yes. Okay. Let's work together.

Looking back through the lens of experience, I let fear get in my way. That is common in any beginning. I learned many lessons the hard way but they helped me create stronger standards and boundaries going forward.

As your probationary period draws to a close, reflect on the relationship. If all is working out well, keep going! If it's feeling difficult, can you pinpoint the pinch? What expectations need to be clarified? What lessons need to be learned from this discomfort? Is this a bump in the road or time to end the relationship?

Remember to look at the struggles with curiosity and not judgment. Struggles often show us what we need to work on. Are the struggles you're feeling a change you need to make in your processes and communications or do you hold unrealistic or non-communicated expectations?

Is the pinch that you are hitting a boundary that requires a hard conversation?

All relationships experience growing pains. If at any point something feels off, talk to your VA about it and see if it can get cleared up. Have the conversation as soon as you are clear enough about the issue. Don't wait until feelings get hurt or you cross a point of no return. If it turns out the fit isn't right, ending things before the relationship turns ugly will save you lots of time in the long run.

If things are going well, woohoo! Celebrate the milestone and keep going. It may be time to add additional tasks or start working on projects that require a bit more trust.

It's impossible to outline all the what-ifs that could come up in a VA-client relationship.

You can't plan for everything. Even after great interviews and a smooth start, red or pink flags can start to emerge.

Communication is super important. Bumps happen when miscommunication happens. Either side of the relationship can feel powerless at times. Articulating feelings and clarifying expectations can go a long way to empowering each person to step into their role with strength and autonomy.

Depend on vs. Dependent on

I love my job. I love helping my clients and seeing them reach their goals. However, I also love being wholly unreachable during my vacation and downtime. Work and life balance is important for both the client and the VA. This allowance of time and space to focus on resting and recharging is good for your mental health and stimulates creativity for your business.

In a Talk It Through session, a client came to me expecting me to validate her exasperation that her VA was not always readily available and didn't respond to communications immediately. The client felt that since she often worked to emergencies, her VA should do the same. I had to disabuse this client of her unrealistic expectations.

It's not uncommon for miscommunications to occur. In the beginning, VAs tend to spend more time learning a new client. It may feel like they are always available because they are adjusting to the new tasks and requests. Over time, as comfort grows and the new client is absorbed into the rest of their workload, the VA may relax back behind their boundaries. This may feel like they aren't as readily available or communicative.

Not all VAs are business and self-aware. They may not think about communicating when their needs change.

My client was butting up against her expectations and her VA's boundaries. It was time to have a hard conversation and clarify expectations.

It is both a blessing and a curse to find a great assistant. When the fit is right, it's very easy to fall into a place of trust and for a client to relinquish total control of the business to their VA. Many clients forget it's still their business and they need to know how to manage it (especially when their VA is unavailable).

Back when I was going through the virtual training program at AssistU, we were taught that our clients should be able to depend on us but not become dependent on us. This is a tricky distinction for a lot of people to make.

To depend on someone means to trust that person will do what you want or expect.

To be dependent on someone means you need that person all the time in order to continue existing or operating.

The distinction is the belief in someone's ability to meet your expectations versus your reliance on that person. A business owner should always be able to step back into their work and power through in the event of their VA's absence or incapacitation.

Here are a couple of tips to keep you from becoming too dependent on your VA:

- **Have a working knowledge of the programs most used for your work:** One of the reasons entrepreneurs and business owners hire a VA is because of their unique skill set and their ability to use tools the client is unfamiliar with. It's unrealistic to know all the ins and outs of a program but ask your VA to give you a brief tutorial on the programs most essential to your work.

- **Use web-based options for seamless transitions:** Many programs are now web-based or have an internet version like Canva, Google Suite for Word, Excel and PowerPoint, Google Drive or Dropbox, etc. Set up a shared folder with links to files, working documents, and passwords so you both have access to what you're working on.

- **Establish a backup VA:** If the work becomes too complicated for you, set up a relationship with a backup VA. This person should have the same needed skill set as your current VA. For example, my colleague LeAnn focuses on more technical aspects while I focus more on design. However, she knows all the same programs that I do and can easily step in to help a client if I need her to.

  Additionally, ask your VA if they have a back-up plan in case of emergency. Add any elements specific to your business into your operating procedures. If you're already working with someone, work together to create your plan.

Many people go into business for themselves for the flexibility of working and playing. Setting up a plan ahead of time makes those play times easier and less fraught with worry. Trust the members of your team but remember that the buck stops with you. It's your business and ultimately, it's up to you to make sure everything runs smoothly with or without your VA.

Relationships don't always last forever. Early in my business, my dad shared some valuable wisdom with me. *"It's okay to fire a client."* At the time, I'd been anxious about working with a client who was a great person but our communication often left me with an upset stomach. I could do the work requested but didn't like it. It was the first time I let a client go because we were not the right fit.

Relationships end for many reasons from both sides. If something feels off, I recommend talking with your VA about it. It may be a communication issue or something small that can be adjusted. If it's not fixable, don't be a ghost! Be professional and have the hard conversation.

Before you have this talk, make sure you have access to all your usernames and passwords, graphics, logos, documents, folders and processes. While I hope any VA you work with will be ethical and above board, I have heard horror stories. Protect yourself!

It may be helpful to budget time and resources for your current VA to train a replacement. However, if there is no overlap, make sure that you can step in and take over any tasks until you find someone.

People come into our lives for a reason, a season, or a lifetime. Not every pairing is meant to last forever and it's okay to let go of a relationship regardless of how good it once was if it no longer feels right.

All of this may seem daunting but your dream is worth the work. You are worth feeling supported and valued. Your business is important. You deserve to be successful and have someone on your team who believes in your business as much as you do.

When it comes to the process of finding, hiring and working with a VA, remember:

There is no perfect time.
You know enough.
Start small.
You got this and, if you don't, I can help!

Recap: Key Points

- **Start Small and Build Trust**

Begin with smaller and more manageable tasks to gauge compatibility, communication, and trust with your VA.

Focus on tasks you procrastinate on or that block progress toward personal or professional goals.

- **Adjusting to Collaboration**

It takes time to release perfectionism and fully delegate tasks to a VA. Gradual hand off of responsibilities can lead to confidence in their capabilities and better collaboration.

- **Reassess and Clarify Expectations**

Regularly evaluate the relationship and address any discomfort or miscommunications. Hard conversations may be necessary to align on boundaries and expectations.

- **Celebrate Milestones and Growth**

At three months, review progress with your VA, celebrate successes, and decide if it's time to delegate more responsibilities. Acknowledge that all relationships evolve and not every match is permanent.

- **Effective Communication**

Overcommunicate initially to manage expectations and minimize mistakes.

Miscommunications can create friction so clarify intentions and changes promptly.

- **Lessons Learned and Adaptation**

Reflect on experiences (both positive and challenging) to adjust and grow together.

Approach challenges with curiosity rather than judgment for continuous improvement.

- **Know When to Let Go**

Not all relationships last. If the fit isn't right, it's okay to part ways amicably.

Letting go can make space for more aligned opportunities.

- **Trust the Process**

There is no perfect time to start working with a VA. Start small, trust your instincts, and grow from there.

Journal Prompts

☺ What small tasks can I start delegating to a VA to build trust and gauge compatibility? How do these tasks align with my goals and what procrastination or blockers do they address?

☺ How am I feeling about gradually handing off responsibilities to my VA?

☺ What challenges or successes do I imagine?

You made it! I hope this book helps you get started on your path to finding the best VA for your needs.

Keep in mind, all the books I mentioned are currently available on Amazon as of this printing but if that changes, you can also check your local library or the retailer of your choice.

You'll find all the handouts and worksheets mentioned on the Resources webpage here: www.ExtraHandsVA.com/resources

And, as I said at the beginning of the book, if you've decided this all too much to do alone, I can help!

Find out more details on working together on my website at www.ExtraHandsVA.com

— Acknowledgments —

When they say it takes a village, I know this to be true. I depended on so many people to help me get this book into the world.

Elizabeth Bercovici - Thank you for being the best book coach and developmental editor extraordinaire. Without your own brand of cheerleading and hand holding, I would have definitely stalled in overthinking.

Jessica Brodkin Webb - Thank you for doing all the work it takes to turn a Word document into an electronic and print book. Thank you also for decades of friendship and support. I'm so glad that the girl I met backstage on *"Yours, Anne"* turned into a lifelong friend.

Susan Wichrowski- Thank you for proofreading in such a quick turnaround! Especially highlighting the commas my dad worked so hard to find that I didn't have the energy to seek out and delete.

Anastacia Brice - Thank you for being my VA mentor, coach and guide. Without your expertise, I would never have created a business that has lasted 20 years. So much of your wisdom permeates through all that I share and believe in. I'm grateful to still call you friend.

Sydney Hubbard - Without you, I would never have been on this journey. Thank you for growing with me through all the ups and downs. Thank you for helping me turn my podcast dream into a reality.

LeAnn Erimli and Bree BV - Thank you for taking the leap with me to turn my idea into our podcast - Hey! Do I Need a VA? You are amazing collaborators and colleagues. I am so grateful you're part of my Tribe.

Rusty Jay Salanio Raymundo - Thank you for bringing your creativity and excitement to my business. From social media graphics to the book cover, I am grateful for your support and genius.

Nicole Dowding - Thank you for bringing your creative skills to the graphics and resources that accompany this book.

To my clients - Thank you for seeing my value and supporting both me and my business growth. A special thank you to Alan Heymann, Jennifer Hart, Caroline Brown, Deepti Gudipati and Barb Hubbard. I am grateful for the gift of supporting you.

To my VA Colleagues - There are so many wonderful VAs in my community. I especially want to send a shoutout to Sandra Trca, Carrie McWherter, Ingrid Carleton, Stephanie Fritz, Antonette Artiz, Terri Piper, Mia Borja, Gillian Zali, Pat Matson, Sonja Chevere, Mika Howard, Ashley Franklin, Jessi Engelke, Chelsea Price, Chelsea Becker, Kat Halushka, Lisa DeToffel, Christine Wilson, Anahita Shahrvini, those I've forgotten to mention and the many more that I've yet to meet.

A special note to Christine Barnes - Thank you for taking time to talk with me about being a VA all those years ago. Without you, I would never have found my calling.

To my Tribe - Beyond friendship, your love, encouragement and support kept me going when my imposter syndrome kicked in. Annie Korn, Barb Hubbard, Bree BV, Charlene Patterson, Espie Lopez, LeAnn Erimli, Jessica Brodkin Webb, Elizabeth Bercovici, Caroline Brown and Janina Goldberg - I am forever grateful for your presence in my life.

To the Writers Group - This book may not be romance but it is a published book. You've been with me on my writer journey for so long. Your wisdom, support and encouragement kept me writing. Shoshana Brown, Janet Tait, Melissa Cutler, Cori Conrad, Marie Andreas, Julie Fine, Juli West, Lynne Mayfield, Lisa Kessler and Natalie Bilski - I'm so grateful for you.

To my family - I could not do any of this without your love, encouragement and support.

Dad - thank you for finding all the errant commas. If any have been missed, it's my mistake. More than that, thank you for always being in my corner. From building a paper mache Utah mountain to scooting out of the way to avoid a thrown stage prop, you've witnessed all my greatest moments (and not-so-great moments). Thank you for being there since day 1.

Damian - I love how you show up for me even when you don't have a clue what I'm talking about. Thank you for growing with me and being my life partner. TDDUP!

Alex and Ash - I love being your mom. Thank you for being the best kids a mom could ask for. I am grateful for your support, love and humor. You brighten my life simply by being in it.

– About the Author –

Rachael Davila is a virtual assistant turned business coach with over 20 years of experience helping entrepreneurs and small business owners take control of their time and their to-do lists. She has been behind the scenes doing everything from managing inboxes to creating systems.

Now, she is on a mission to help business owners like you stop juggling everything and start building the business (and life) they really want.

After years of helping clients scale, Rachael realized it was time to walk her own talk. She transitioned from a busy VA to a coach who shows others how to delegate, build strong systems, and stop getting stuck in the "I can do it all" mindset. Her approach? Make things easier and not harder because building something great shouldn't mean burning out.

When she is not coaching or helping clients streamline their business, you can probably find her with a cup of coffee working on her next big idea or spending time with her family. Rachael is all about balance and she believes that you don't have to do it all alone to grow your business and thrive.

www.ingramcontent.com/pod-product-compliance
Lightning Source LLC
Chambersburg PA
CBHW060932220326
41597CB00020BA/3518